THE
PINEAPPLE
THEORY

Steve "Mr. Pineapple" Mathieu

CONTENTS

ABOUT THE AUTHOR

Picture by: Anthony "with a camera" Scrocco

Steve *"Mr. Pineapple"* Mathieu is born and raised in Montreal, Canada. French is its native language, and he wrote The Pineapple Theory series in English. He manages Loss Prevention & Safety for 25+ years in retail & supply chain. He is a firm ambassador of Culture and Core Values. When COVID-19 impacted life on Earth, he took full benefit of the forced leisure time sacrifice to reflect – make peace – and became prosperous which trigger its purpose.

S. Mathieu is known for being passionate, for his determination, and for being like the fruit; positively authentic.

The only thing you'll be missing from your reading is Mr. Pineapple's beautiful French-Canadian accent!

Everyone is invited to contact him on LinkedIn or at: thepineappletheory.ca

"It's all about people with Mr. Pineapple."
- *Readers of The Pineapple Theory*

"You will aways harvest what you planted."

Steve "Mr. Pineapple" Mathieu

DEDICATION

To YOU, the reader, the human, who chose to harvest a book of The Pineapple Theory, push your curiosity passed the cover page, the critics, and soon, passed the introduction.

A pineapple positive authenticity in a blur of biases

Throughout Earth timeline, the book industry established & influenced frugal conditioning with how books should be written and presented, feeding an emotional perfection that does not exist. A blur of biases around becoming one of several inner battles to keep my pineapple balance on my inner foundation.

When shopping for pineapple fruit, the fruit's positive authenticity does not stop a customer. When shopping for a book, The Pineapple Theory (TPT) is intended to be like a pineapple fruit on the shelf. The big difference is that the pineapple exceptional authenticity is known & admired since the 17th century, and TPT, still new. Since 2020 I'm swimming counterflow which inspired and is at the origin of my text titled: *The determination of a salmon,* speaking of our inner roar with my complete theory titled, *The Pineapple Theory.*

I'm fully aware that the manuscripts of TPT books are not emotionally perfect for everyone, and it is intended to be that way with the purpose of educating readers at being comfortable with what is uncomfortable. Like pineapples on a pizza, not everything is for everyone, meaning that one must keep it sweet inside/out.

Because everything in life is a pattern, TPT books have patterns such as each book starts with this text, starts and builds-on the same chapter title: *The Management of Emotions,* and sometimes they share a reader's testimonial from their reading experience with the purpose of breaking other readers biases with an industry boxed expectation felt like bullying.

Imagine one voicing "MOOstache" instead of moustache. One has the choice to understand or to voluntarily not understand even if they do. An honest mistake that could be an awareness about one's moustache has a nose booger!

One of several messages shared with TPT is that in life, there is no emotional perfection. The reading of TPT must focus on the messages shared, not with the bias of "how it's written" resulting in turning down a positive purpose. Ones' bias is one seeking around instead of within.

The positive win over my inner battle as follows: When life gives you lemons, define as a negative force, I sell them, and I purchase a pineapple. When potential readers and agencies choose turning down a purpose to only provide & encourage what is an emotional perfection from their emotional point of view, it is what it is. I will find my way like I do because life is a do-it-yourself project, there's no gain without pain, and you must believe to achieve.

One reading TPT must read, read, and read again what the books are sharing to culture a growth continuum within. It follows the following quotations from Earth timeline:

Socrates
Employ your time in improving yourself by other men's writings so that you shall come easily by what others have labored hard for.

Plato
Writing is the geometry of the soul.

Epictetus
Don't just say you have read books. Show that through them you have learned to think better, to be a more discriminating and reflective person.

In the emotional illusions with *life & time*, when one's blur of biases is their roadblock, one is walking around with a nose booger on their MOOstache!

Be positively curious and when reading The Pineapple Theory, focus & cultivate the messages. Read – Think – Relate.

Feed positively your roots

Master the art

Be inspired
Be inspiring

THE
MANAGEMENT
OF
EMOTIONS

Planet Earth has a master shell to protect life:
Its inner sweetness.

Earth quality of life can be defined as:
Emotions!

Earth quality of life – emotions – can be defined by how
negative & positive they are experienced.

The influencers for negative & positive emotions are:
Humans!

Emotions, 24/7, every human has them and feels them. It is like a never-ending rollercoaster which contains moments of goodness and displeasure. Society's emotions are another rollercoaster, a wild ride. We could say it is two rollercoasters crossing path frequently. Many things happen every day to everyone making the management of emotions a challenge.

- A portion of society is controlled by their negative emotions.
- A portion of society turns negative emotions into violence.
- A portion of society chooses to be blind to what are facts. (Cannot handle the truth)
- Political decisions will be felt as both positive and negative.
- The media will provide positive emotions to a society and sometimes, feed the negative with negative.
- Social media can contain misleading information, "fake news," and personal diary to be seen by all in a life comparison. All these trigger various emotions.
- A portion of society will experience satisfactory emotions by creating traumatic emotions to others.
- And much more can be stated.

Based on the *Pareto principle* (the 80/20 principle), the above list may involve an extreme 20% of society resulting 80% challenge in remaining positive. The reality is, 100% of society will feel and manage emotions differently.

The objective of this topic is to inform the readers of the challenges they will likely face due to human' emotions, suggest perspectives, principles, concepts and tools to you, the leader of your life.

An exceptionally long time ago

A topic generating various emotions is religious beliefs. This section of the book IS NOT to be Religious. Rather, the goal is to take a perspective trip back in time and, at a light speed, bring us back to now.

Let us remove from our mind all names and stories used in religious beliefs and work with the raw concepts provided in many of them.

Raw concepts from religious beliefs provide guidelines of behaviors and manageable methods for positiveness leading humans to behave with best practices between them. We could think the mission was to establish a positive Culture with Core Values such as: Trust, Respect and Communication which are valuable if there's absence of love.

Globally, every type of religious concept led to a positive Culture with Core Values. Each village and town had a representative to help and guide the population to maintain a solid foundation of each concept. There was even at least one day of the week dedicated to it, with an assigned location to congregate, discuss and provide support. The idea of life after death was used to influence Best Practices by all.

As years passed, the population increased, some individuals took an opposite direction to feed their own emotions regardless of others, generating an overload of negative emotions, dominating, and dividing society with how to manage their emotions with skin color, gender, sexual orientation. In addition, darker challenges came in play; alcohol, drugs, gambling, money, and sexuality are some examples.

Through time, the rollercoaster of emotions became an intense ride. Books of rules with punishments were created in the attempt to influence order and best practices in society.

One of the challenges of today is at achieving an experience of general harmony in society and the list of actions that would most likely influence this objective may be extensive and be a complicated recipe.

What if how you market & sell yourself, products, and services could positively influence and cultivate more harmony in society?

Per a philosophy of The Pineapple Theory
Humans are responsible for nearly all problems and they are the solution for everything. Be a positive solution.

THE PINEAPPLE SEED

The BIG Bang of Marketing!

Daily, everywhere, marketing surround us, and its environment becoming us.

The core principle of marketing follows a deep understanding of humans' primitive behaviors, their emotions, and their psychology. It's conditioning, manipulation, and humans are emotionally hooked without knowledge and in the last half of 2022, Earth experienced The BIG Bang of Marketing unrolling a Royal red carpet leading to 10 January 2023.

From approximately 1550-1800 A.D was the emergence of the absolute monarch, meaning, the Monarchy era of Earth timeline. The concept still lives today, and it means BIG business because it feeds a dream. A couple's wedding is a sweet obvious example. For most cultures, a one-day event for which a couple is receiving Royal attention and admiration providing a feeling-a-like. My preferred example is when a customer or client is receiving a Royal treatment, meaning that they are given an amazing experience.

Through time, several TV channels have proven how humans are voyeurs along with a need for drama of others' lives by showcasing reality TV shows. Lock of groups of people, film them 24/7, and let's admire their drama and lifestyle. If nothing happens, organizers will initiate drama to feed a show. In the last half of 2022, The BIG Bang of Marketing was as followed.

It started with the announcement about the memoirs (book) from a member of the British Royal family scheduled for release on 10 January 2023. The announcement followed a suggested communication process shared with my title of The Pineapple Theory.

It started with a periodic reminder followed with the Drill Down. Daily, everybody was hearing about it. Through time, society is voyeur about the Royal family. It's an odd emotion to wonder: Do they live like us?

A major streaming platform was a partner with this strategy and released a short series feeding society with January 10th launch along with the media of the world speaking about it, daily. The last sprint of the strategy was a continuum of the drill down by sharing "leaks" from the book stuffing society voyeurism about the Royal family. Once launched, a large portion of society was hungry for it, then, the silence mode because the results were in the bank.

The BIG Bang of Marketing is worthy of its name because the book was already translated into several languages for a Worldwide launch, and life within the Royal Family has inspired humans for centuries. To support a Return On Investment (ROI), a BIG Bang Marketing roadmap was built to create a worldwide buzz using the most influential voice available: Media.

The leverage of what is popular – The leverage about what has a social notoriety – Finding partners to invest in a BIG marketing scheme – Creating a worldwide buzz – and inspiring the most influential voice (Media) to speak about it therefore increasing their ratings leading to pocket more from their media services leading to January 10's launch to become a worldwide best seller, was quite a cocktail creating a blur in the emotional illusions with *life & time*.

Coaching with the Extreme Obvious is a valuable concept suggested with my theory and it has the purpose of coaching and persuading. The BIG Bang of Marketing is an *extreme obvious* about marketing because major companies such as Pepsi, Coca Cola, Mc Donald's, Apple and more follows the *extreme obvious* from your reading. They are global, they have deep pockets, and their marketing is intended to keep them on top of mind when we are in need to purchase a product falling under their category. Even more important, and this will be read again later, these big brands don't truly sell a product with their marketing – rather – they sell a story, an emotion because humans don't just feel their emotions, they built them. Meaning that they earn people's heart, then they earn everything else.

A perspective about this view using psychology, is as follows: Society is intensively exposed to their marketing and their brand is hooked in the non-conscious thought (un-conscious is you prefer), meaning that when you pick that brand it's without thinking about it, also meaning it became a natural choice to make. It's a *mere exposure*.

The *mere exposure effect* suggests that people develop a preference for things simply because they are familiar, meaning repeated exposure to a stimulus, even if fleeting, can lead to increased liking or preference for that stimulus.

Back to reality

The meaning of this exceptional book is to inspire you with realistic leads to solutions with the purpose of marketing & selling yourself, products, and services. The ultimate result is achieving your goals while providing a Royal experience to your audience meaning, earning their heart first with the welcoming hospitality of a pineapple.

My expertise is in mindset, performance, and emotional control. I will share reality with you to keep focus with what you can control, including when risky decisions must be taken, and it is important to burst through the emotional illusions with *life & time.*

I must share, if you truly wish to upgrade the value of your investment from your reading, the following titles are premium options for you because they are exceptionally set apart in the Self-Help category.

What to expect with this book?

I remember when COVID-19's first wave swamped everyone requiring staying home. A few TV and movie personalities would post on social media a motivational *"ish"* and comforting *"ish"* message to their followers, and the world, as follow: *"It will be alright."*

For them staying home was "alright" because they reside in mansions equipped with what the average "joe" of society needs outside their apartment, condo, or home. Similarly, it's like books teaching how to become a salesperson. It's easy to create emotional illusions and promises if the author is calling themselves an "expert" and has never had their boots on the field feeling the real hustle. An expert must be someone who has experienced all possible mistakes. Daily requires persuasion to make us a salesperson. It is true in your personal life, in the workplace, and as an entrepreneur. Take time to reflect and write in a notebook 3 to 5 scenarios that once required you to become a salesperson. What was your approach? What were your emotions? How did you close the deal? Let's think about this:

- You detected an opportunity to improve the process in the workplace and needed to sell a solution.
- You wished to pilot a project in the workplace and needed a budget.
- You and your friends could not agree which restaurant to go to. How did you close the deal by selling the location you had in mind?
- How about vacation with family? You had a destination in mind, your partner another one. Have you closed the deal with your thoughts?

I share that life is an experience and one of 15 fundamental anchors with my theory is to experience like a *guinea pig*. Since 2020, I've been spending hours writing words and speaking about what an emotional experience is in my books. But let us bear in mind that our life experience could be a resume because we completed life projects, we sold ideas, obtained budget, surmounted and succeeded with several ups & downs when completing our projects, and more. Your life experience requires skills, tools, and practice. I will speak about it later, but not all authors about how to become a salesperson builds an emotional illusion, and those who don't are the ones I suggest considering reading.

Like me, you are likely boots on the field (I share field for a pineapple plantation instead of ground) dealing directly with your audience, current & future clients, often in-person or virtually. This book is written from my *guinea pig* experience with boots on my pineapple plantation, always experiencing several emotional ups & downs, and welcoming the daily hustles with the purpose of making a positive and fruitful valuable contribution in people's life meaning, cultivating more positiveness within to live more "pineHapply", together.

Like opening Google Earth, you first see Earth. Then, if you zoom-in a little, about 1 to 3 names start showing and yet, it remains a big and large picture. This book shares a big picture, that little extra zoom. Because we must always navigate our boat of life with more than one anchor, I am not serving you with a luxurious extreme close-up because the goal is for you to use all the tools to think for yourself. They are seeds for thought because you are the farmer, and you will always harvest what you have planted.

My tip for you when reading; highlight, add sticky notes, and journal. Avoid rushing your reading meaning, following a section or chapter, Pause – Think – and Relate by taking notes. Give a shape to your new ideas and insights, give a different shape to your roadblock, and always seek for controllable solutions.

With your notes, build bridges with your vision, products, or services. Daily, everyone is like a salesperson, everyone is required to persuade, and everyone is their own brand, image, and shadow. You attract from who you are within. You are reading this book, and you may be within the process of launching, you may have already launched, or you may be already successful and are *positively curious* to discover refreshing perspectives. Or, what if you have a leadership position in the workplace and are curious at pineapple picking perspectives that can be modeled and applied, making your business culture always thrive better? My preferred, what if you are reading to become a better leader, a better human, by always becoming an improved thriving version of yourself?

Like a sport athlete, the best is the one practicing all the time, and even if they are a master, they keep learning and practicing. It gives volume to another philosophy of The Pineapple Theory.

Masters, they always keep learning and practicing.

I remember in the workplace enjoying a great conversation of thoughts with a manager. I was learning about their ambitions and hopes, then it led them to openly share with me their fear about the idea of becoming an entrepreneur. I must share, make people talk about what passionate them and you'll witness a pineHapply shining person.

You may have once had the courage to exit the comfortable luxury of a bi-weekly pay deposit in your bank account to suddenly wonder if you will make enough money this month to pay the bills and eat as an entrepreneur. Because making people think is what I do, even if philosophy can be thought provocative, a walked away from the conversation by sharing the following pineapple seed for thoughts in their mind:

"If you can find the right solutions for someone else pocket - don't fear becoming an entrepreneur - you will find the right solutions for your own pocket. In fact, if you can wake up early for someone's dream, you can do it for your own."

Because there's no consistency with perfection in life, what you learn from books is not perfect standardization working exactly by how it's expressed. In perspective with our timeline, questions were the same, but the answers changed. Things in life hardly happen the way you'll like them to happen – therefore – keep peace by accepting how they happen. Like in the field of customers service, it's a mistake dealing with an escalation with a process that looked like a one-fit-all. YOU are positively the solution and expect to fail a few times. Though, I suggest engraving the following in your mind: If you've failed, fixed, learned, and did not repeat, you have not failed, you have successfully risen. You may experience bad starts but it doesn't mean a bad finish. From several fails stories which led to finalizing my theory, I share the following motivational message: : FAIL stands for First Attempt In Learning and it's never the end because END stands for, Effort Never Dies.

Never forget that pineapples don't grow with magic beans. When using new tools for the first time, there's an adaptation period until you become comfortable with them. It's like self-growth; it requires patience to become someone we've never been before. What greatly assist growth is to always stand up and improve your processes and learn from your failures. It's life's *Law of Balance*. Meaning, you start over with experience, then you harvest positiveness from what was felt negatively. Allow me to share the following perspective, also explaining why I often market that The Pineapple Theory being an addition to one's life & leadership recipe.

Recipes in cookbooks are from the author's/chef's taste and solution. If you follow the recipe exactly from your reading, you will likely enjoy the result. What if the recipe shares adding one pineapple ring, and you choose to experiment by adding 2 pineapple rings? The result will be like *Schrodinger's Cat* meaning that you will love it, hate it, or maybe both. The lesson is that you tried and experimented with it making you way ahead of many people who never tried anything. What I suggest is that I have done with The Pineapple Theory, and because we are 8 billion humans on Earth, everybody experiences their emotions differently, and human tribe by commonality. Meaning that the tools from your reading, you will need to adapt by using them along with your recipe fitting the tribe, or niche, fitting your product/s or service/s. For the rest of your reading, let us assume that you have several products and services.

My purpose with The Pineapple Theory is adding a pineapple to people's life, leadership, and business recipes, inspire and cultivate positivity within and around using philosophy, psychology, and wisdom. It serves to always understand more than we think we do by seeking the rare treasure of self-awareness. If I had to share one sentence summarizing not only this book, but all the books I have released to date assisting readers at always giving themselves and others of their own self-growth transformation is as follows:

You will always harvest what you planted, like a pineapple!

Let the sweet journey begin!

Surveyed by The Pineapple Theory

To make money:
Does it take money or is it about who you know?

75%: It's about who you know.
25%: It takes money.

.

MINDSET

Overview

For many, a salesperson is not a cue for positive emotions because several salespersons exhibit emotional patterns felt like an emotional fisherman. In psychology, there's a concept referred to as *pattern disruption* and it suggests an unexpected or unusual event that interrupts a person's established thought processes, behaviors, or habitual responses, potentially leading to a shift in perspective or behavior.

Like this chapter becoming page 1 instead of 16. It's a *pattern disruption* voluntarily inserted, and it hides a philosophic statement.

In life, your mindset is a must and might just be your most important and most powerful tool when marketing & selling *yourself, products, and services* because it's like a weapon to overcome obstacles. A positive mindset is what I like to realistically call *optimism*. It's what you can control because feeling pain, fear, stress, and anxiety about what you cannot control in life is a waste of your emotional energy and it disturb your focus. Instead, seek within because you can always control the home you've built within yourself. Let's apply life's *Law of Balance,* another fundamental anchor from my theory, as follows:

🍓 What if you could turn a disadvantage into an advantage?
🍓 What if you could turn a liability into an asset?
🍓 What if a failure could become a success, and your defeat into victory?

 A love *pattern disruption* example of mine is such a cliché: A person asks*, "Hey, how's it going?"* and the answer is, *"I'm ok, thanks."*

And that is it! It is such a classic pattern for humans that I personally enjoy disrupting it. The observed reactions are a social experiment. This simple pattern – social cliché – truly speaks how our non-conscious thought work meaning that it's a natural conditioned behavior voiced/acted without thinking about it, until something disrupts it and there's a delay before our conscious thought is poked by sending the following message to our non-conscious thought: *"Hey, you did not made sense!"*

Believe it because it's true, there are people I never talked before and when I share a *"hello",* they non-consciously respond, *"I'm ok, thanks."* There's a function about human's brain that "kinda" predict the next step based on several common experienced patterns. Beautifully about this is the function of our eyes compared to a body cam. The engineering of our eyes will predict an upcoming sequence nearly eliminating or reducing what a body cam doesn't, meaning that if you run, the body cam shows a shaky view and your eyes a more stable view. I share with my books that the eyes are useless if the mind is blind because it speaks in perspective the prediction function of humans' brain. It is an emotional illusion created by our own. My *"hello"* was actually *"Hi, how are you TODAY?"* DATA collected from my social experiment suggest the following three types of people:

Person 1
They never realized what just happened and I simply moved on.

Person 2
When their conscious thought spoke to their non-conscious thought, a frozen reaction is observed, and nothing more is done about it.

Person 3
Same as person 2, but they will respond back with an answer suited to the question.

As a salesperson, leader in the workplace, and citizen of Earth, listen to understand. Anchor the following psychological information in your mind because when marketing & selling yourself, products, and services, it is the *platinum* of pineapples, that one thing that many say is obvious and yet, they did not get the results and influence they deserved.

You see, people are like books. Many see the cover only; many only listen and believe the critics. Limited are those reading the introduction and even less positively curious knowing about the content. Meaning that, be the *pattern disruptor* about what many negatively believe about salespeople. The more you read this book, the more you will understand that consistency is a must with everybody, even those who don't deserve it because they need it the most and when you experience a bad day, no one should pay the price for it. In fact, hurt people don't have to hurt people. One bad day is not one bad life.

About the negative emotion triggered by salespeople, who truly enjoys the following?

- Receiving a cold call when you never give your phone number.
- Feeling forced to purchase or forced to take a decision.
- Hearing about the out-of-date and overused selling methods.

Salespeople are compared by many with a metaphor of The Pineapple Theory shared erlier, meaning an *emotional fisherman*. This is not good because the *emotional fisherman* is someone thinking for themselves.

What I suggest about a mindset is that it defines one's character and for many, it defines the purity of their soul. Like employees choosing their leader in the workplace, your future client must like *you* before they like your *products and services*. Earn people's heart, then earn everything else.

One's mindset is simple words – impactful like copywriting – shared by others when speaking about one. You never know who, and who speaks to whom. I personally view that your life & leadership philosophy is the roots because it must embody you, and your mindset is you as a farmer meaning cultivating and nurturing the seed influencing a growth continuum, leading to how others will *think/act/speak* about what is ready for harvest. I will share more about my pineapple plantation of thoughts about this topic for each of the following mindset. Ready…mind…set…pineapple!

People sell to people / People buy from people

The Pineapple Theory is all about it by sharing what is beyond the word important because it is the emotional value of a Human-2-Human (H2H) relation and connection. It is powerful in your personal life, when leading a team in the workplace, and as an entrepreneur when meeting new people and dealing with clients. A H2H is also defined as people sell to people and people buy from people.

Who you are is the key to success because you are positively the solution. If provide me with the privilege of reading The Pineapple Theory book, you will discover the philosophical thought about having our 3 faces connected to the same roots. BE YOU. People prefer to follow someone with a heart rather than their title. People will always remember how you made them feel. You will greatly benefit from being similar and common like your collaborators and clients. When you listen to understand, and when you see to observe, what you hear and see provides you with several leads for conversational ice breakers and it establishes *similarity* with one.

In psychology, *similarity principle* is a key part of *Gestalt Psychology,* and it suggests that our brains tend to group elements that share visual characteristics like color, shape, or size, perceiving them as unified whole rather than separate entities.

One of the 3 core fundamentals of The Pineapple Theory is called, *be positively curious*, and it gives volume by making others speak, by giving them the stage, and saving all information will amazingly serve you with several of the remaining mindset, insights, and leads to solution from this book.

How you will make others feel starts with how you feel, meaning that it starts with your ability to experience positive emotions even on more challenging days or weeks. How you see yourself in your heart is how you will see the world and act with it. You are your own cure, your thoughts are like a *placebo*, meaning that a beautiful day starts with a beautiful mindset. Each day you wake up, you have a critical decision to make, do you choose to have a good or bad day? This is important because we all have our daily inner ups & downs.

In psychology, it's referred to as, *ideomotor theory,* and it suggests that anticipating the sensory consequences of a movement can automatically trigger an associated motor response, implying that actions are initiated by the idea of their effects rather than a conscious decision.

With the analogy of the pineapple, we all need our inner storms. It waters the soil making a new fresh pineapple grow for everyone, including yourself, to enjoy. Nevertheless, when an inner storm or simply a cloud is passing by no one around you should become a victim. I can't stress the following enough because they are highly valuable at harvesting the best about yourself; the 3 fundamentals of The Pineapple Theory; *Be positively Curious – The Emotional Batteries – Seek Within*. Learn about them, practice them, master them. When a black belt pineapple, being in-control of your emotions, in-balance, and with harmony builds self-confidence and it becomes positive energy for yourself and for others to enjoy

Love – Time – Health

Fruitfully completing the H2H recipe is by adding the following mindset which is also one of the 15 fundamental anchors of my theory, and it will follow up through your reading: Love – Time – Health.

This mindset is valuable for yourself, and others. In life, no matter if it's from your own thoughts or from others, if something is not giving you with at least one of the 3, move on.

In your position, how you will choose to *think/act/speak* must give Love – Time – Health and, it is often bridged *(framed)* with the following three: Relief a pain – Save a fear – Realistically cultivate their ambitions & hopes.

I must share, you may find the following manipulative, but understanding humans' emotions better, their psychology, and how to bridge it with rationality is a powerful combination in sales, when leading a team in the workplace, and within society. All originate from the following fundamental anchor of my theory: Desire – Motive – Opportunity.

When helping others by giving Love – Time – Health, you are putting them first, and you are demonstrating respect and concern for their needs and desires. Your communication is impactful, persuasive, and will reach people's heart. When becoming agile with this fundamental anchor, it becomes an enhance ability, it is you providing positive energy, positive thoughts, and positive solutions. When people are emotionally moved with positiveness, they purchase. What you understand and can use better than the average requires to be from a place of good like a pineapple farmer, and it gives life to the following philosophy of The Pineapple Theory: Be Kind & Truthful and life will be Fruitful.

That's an important responsibility, it cultivates emotions within others, and those emotions will be remembered. Those emotions will be given back to you. In psychology, it's referred to as *reciprocity effect,* which is often seen in models like reciprocal determinism or reciprocal effects models, suggests that two or more factors mutually influence each other, creating a dynamic and cyclical relationship where each factor both causes and is caused by the others.

I often share that I'm the *guinea pig* of my own theory meaning that I had, and still do, put myself in many situations with the purpose to experience the pains, the fears, and the ambitions & hopes. When I'm the *guinea pig,* my inspiration peaks. If humans' love stories and require persuasion, if humans' emotions are the core, being the *guinea pig* becomes inspiring, and the messages are leaner with impactful copywriting and speaking. Even when I build a new product requiring adding external services, I must experience it like a client to make sure I can speak about it efficiently and provide quality products and services from how I market & sell myself.

It was shared earlier and is worthy to be reminded because it is valuable for you, and you can inspire others with this message. Feeling pain, fear, stress, anxiety about what you cannot control in life is a waste of your emotional energy – instead - seek within because you can control your inside and there's nothing more beautiful than realizing just how strong you are with the strength of positive thinking dominating a negative thinking.

🍍   What if you could turn a disadvantage into an advantage?
🍍   What if you could turn a liability into an asset?
🍍   What if a failure could become a success, and your defeat into victory?

With the purpose of servicing as a tool, you easily can assess your emotional & logical thinking with the following controllables: Your words, thoughts, response, self-awareness & consciousness, and how you treat others is 100% your responsibility.

Relief pain

Per a philosophy of The Pineapple Theory, Love the pineapple you have now before life teaches you to live with the Ananas you have lost. What I also suggest with my theory is that humans are more reactive than proactive.

Later in this book, I will share valuable insights to be cultivated at keeping yourself and your future client more positive when pain or fear is experienced. Often, people will not make a change until they are necessary or unless they feel a sense of urgency. With my 25+ years of corporate experience, it is painful to hear the following nonsense excuse by senior leaders because they are reactive instead of proactive: *"It never happened before so why will it happen now?"*

Sadly, many are waiting for life to force them to change when in fact, life is the one waiting for them to change. They will share excuses such as, they don't have the budget, now is not the time or it's not their priority, or they don't need it. I once heard the following and found it inspiring; if you truly do not wish to spend, why are you stepping inside a shopping mall?

When there's pain, psychologically, their emotions dominate and become their emotional illusion with *life & time*, meaning that their emotions are no longer bridged with their rationale. Here's an example:

One could proactively purchase an air conditioner for their residence, but they don't need it for now because the temperature is comfortable, or they don't have the budget for it, or they don't have the time for it. Until a heat wave hits, and they have not slept for 3 nights. Because there's pain, their emotions take over and magically, there's time and money. Another fundamental anchor from the conclusions of my theory refers to this behavior as, *egocentric theory,* a powerful tool to understand humans for persuasion.

In psychology, *egocentric theory* is primarily associated with Jean Piaget's developmental psychology, it suggests that young children tend to believe that everyone sees the world from their own perspective, essentially thinking that their thoughts, feelings, and experiences are the same as everyone else's, placing themselves at the center of their universe and unable to fully grasp another person's point of view; in simpler terms, it means children believe, "everyone thinks like me."

For marketing and as a salesperson, understanding that relieving a pain can give Love – Time – Health means that you will be an opportunist.

Manipulation with persuasion techniques will trigger the emotion of pain followed by the solution defined as your products, and services. I call it being a Troublemaker for the following reasons.

Reflecting about my theory, I remind the following to readers: You can complain or have solutions, but not both. In perspective, my work's purpose is to challenge readers at being the solution with themselves. Now, reflecting about my decades at supporting companies, I'm successful if I identify problems because they will become a seed for solutions and continuous improvement. And that's how this book speaks at the exact moment you are reading because you don't choose a product to sell; you choose a problem to solve. Meaning, start with a problem.

The last sentence gives value to the following fundamental anchor: Save a fear, relief a pain, realistically support ambitions & hopes.

Maybe it's a problem in an industry, or with a business model, or a daily problem people need solved. Once a problem is found, turn that problem into a question, then come up with an answer to that question. What I suggest is don't jump to a product but find a simple logical solution to the problem you've chosen.

Then, find a product that gets the customer from the problem to your solution, and please do the right thing because if you can't find a problem, make one! This process is how you find great product ideas because theoretically, all creations have the purpose to solve one's pain and save their fear.

Here is a generic example
"You know about [problem here]? It inspired us to invent (or create) [solution here] and follow an experiment [study and/or DATA as proof].

Here's a *guinea pig* example
Approximately 2KM away from my *pineapple casa* is a franchise Lebanese restaurant and I am their customer since they launched. People love their chicken from the stick with their garlic sauce. Operated by a family of 7 (father and children), I can share that trust was established a few months following their launch and one day, I noticed packs of gum next to the register. Immediately in my mind, I told myself, *"Genius,"* because they are in an industrial area. Seconds later, with a laughing friendly approach, I commented to one of the owners, *"I bet you sell out daily"*. They did, and because the name of the restaurant is from a chain, all additions to current standards requires approval from the owners. I guided them with the

following mindset and pitch if they were to be challenge about their pack of gum initiative: *"You are relieving a pain, the one from the garlic sauce."* Their initiative was influenced by this simple mindset, from a simple solution to the owners, and it became an official program across the network.

The *As Seen on TV* ads are pure magic because they are truly an *Extreme Obvious* we can learn from. A 1-minute ad will make you build the emotional pain and/or fear about a daily routine task and present the solution with a *cheezy* approach and theatrical acters feeling relief – and they've never been so happy - using the solution.

Bear in mind that people respond more positively when they are shared what they will lose or miss out on rather than what they stand to gain. This persuasion technique creates pain, or fear, and you are positively the solution. How you approach your communication can influence or convince a person to do what you wish for with reference to in psychology as, *Loss Aversion,* and it suggests that people tend to feel the pain of a loss more strongly than the pleasure of an equivalent gain, leading them to be more motivated to avoid losses than to acquire gains.

In the 90s, a psychologist did an experiment and discovered the *Loss Aversion* psychological phenomenon. To sum it up with the following sentence: Human beings are twice as sensitive to loss as to gain. Example:

If I give you a hundred dollars, you'll be happy. But if I take it back, you will be twice as unhappy as you were at the beginning making Trials a valuable consideration because it also implied referred to in psychology as, *The Ikea Effect,* and it suggests that people tend to place a higher value on products they partially created or assembled themselves, even if the product is objectively the same as one that was fully assembled. Another example could be as follows.

If you want to convince a friend to start working out with you, don't tell them that it will make them fit. Tell them that they will get fatter and fatter, and it will be much harder to lose weight afterwards. Your friend will understand that now is their best time to lose weight easily and if they don't work out, they'll lose the chance.

Loss Aversion can become a manipulative technique when telling someone they're not ready "for it" because people hate being told they can't have something by making them doubt themselves. Picture you're in a negotiation and you say, *"I'm not sure you're ready for this deal. It's a big commitment."* Within, you've anchored, and the person becomes hooked. Because their ego has been poked, within, they are arguing, trying to prove you wrong and likely feel desperate to show they are ready.

Speaking of the *Ikea Effect*, it can be emerged with what is referred to in psychology as, the *generation effect,* and it suggests that actively producing information during encoding, rather than passively reading it, leads to significantly better memory performance later on.

Meaning that how you market & sell yourself, products, and services like a pineapple can become exceptionally unforgettable. Have you ever noticed ads that ask questions, show puzzles, or leave blanks for viewers to fill in?

The *generation effect* is tricking the audience to fill in the blanks on purpose, and brands that do this often stick in people's mind because their message turns into their achievement. When people find the answers themselves, they accomplished something by themselves, and they are more likely to remember it.

Save a fear!

Because you cannot predict a future that does not exist, what happens if a deadly accident happens to you tomorrow? Do you have proper insurance providing the support needed for your family? Do you wish to provide psychological safety to your family with the support needed if this had to happen?

Because persuasion often requires an *Extreme Obvious,* I am currently completing the edit phase of this book, and the 2023 Ocean Gate event happened. Many can relate to it because it was spoken worldwide by the media and every event or story pushed worldwide by the media is volume to your storytelling journal.

The human brain is a fascinating, complex and yet beautifully engineered artwork. Part of the limbic system is an almond-shaped part called, *the amygdala*, and it governs our reactions to events that are important for our survival. Meaning that it stimulates fear to warn us of imminent danger.

Creating fear is an emotional manipulation pushing one to act. Creating fear to inspire a bias for action speaks Earth timeline meaning that humans are pushed to act by giving them fear. It surcharges your future client's mind by making their emotion of fear take control. Coincidentally, it turns out that your products and services are a solution to saving fear. It's one more reason why acting from a place of good is your responsibility because it's a powerful enhance ability.

Your future client can feel fear at the idea of trying something new. Humans love their comfort zone and often, they forget how they created it. What I suggest is to make Love – Time – Health shine with studies about your products and services, use the power of storytelling because people love being inspired by other stories. About a story speaking about why and a problem you wish to solve:

🍓   What was one's starting point such as what was their comfort zone along with pain & fear?
🍓   What were the ups & downs of the products or services through the change?
🍓   Lastly, what was their success story?

Each niche likely requires their own story. Remember the following about storytelling. For centuries humans have spent money to watch a movie at the theater. Movies always positively end like success stories. What people truly pay for and are curious about is how it got to this positive conclusion meaning, the process, the story.

Your audience fear needs to be saved with a free trial. Give a trial enough time so it becomes a new behavior for your future client. I probably have read my books over 100 times when writing this book and I share about the *21/90 days change management concept*, meaning that you commit for 21 days, then keep going for another 90 days to truly make it a natural new behavior, comfort zone, engraved in your non-conscious like a habit. *Loss aversion* is in motion. I am not telling you how many days it will take when defining your trial program (if you are planning for one), but I am sharing with you leads to finding your own solutions. Have you ever noticed the pattern with, *"try it for 30 days and if you're not satisfied, get your money back"*?

Some are pushing their limits to save a fear with the following: *"We will refund double what you paid."* The food industry, such as restaurants and grocery stores, are also a tasty example of saving fear, meaning the one about trying something on the spot. The German have a proverb speaking of this: *Forge the iron while it's warm.*

For example, you are grocery shopping and there's a sample table. Or, at the restaurant, the classical pattern is a must to feed a need. The pattern is enjoying an appetizer, main meal (entrée), followed by dessert and coffee. Good business for a restaurant is when the classical pattern is in-full therefore, how to prevent a client self-creating a *pattern disruption* while providing them with an experience keeping the classic pattern in motion?

For every stage of the roadmap, the staff member will ask if you desire the next step by asking, for example: *"How about trying our delicious homemade desserts?"* I have not experienced the following for some time now, but I remember some restaurant would literally come to your table following your main meal with their dessert offering in front of you, meaning that you can physically see it, smell it, and taste it.

That's powerful for one's emotion taking over their logic because if they decline a dessert, they will miss the satisfactory enjoyment in-full of the sweetness they tasted. When many like me speak about your clients' experience, it is like selling sizzle, not meat. Like a coffee shop making expressos like any other coffee shop but, you get a unique artwork when served one. How about Starbuck with a personal note on the glass.

<u>Cultivate their ambitions & hopes.</u>

The Law of Balance is one more fundamental anchor with my theory because it's a daily & life reality. Pain and fear are negative emotions. Now, let us work with your future client's positive emotions: Their ambitions and hopes.

Challenges when dealing with pain and fear are their resistance. The positive thing about one's ambitions and hopes is that it can feel like a smooth ride on the river of life. Word of cautious, be a pineapple farmer. Be kind & truthful and life will be fruitful. Meaning that as a salesperson, do not take advantage of one's ambitions and hopes because you are thinking for yourself only of making a quick sale. True in a saturated market because the more saturated, the more scammers there are. I remember at the beginning of my professional career, I was full of ambitions, and my managers had the same poor and abusive way of feeding it, and I absolutely needed to burst through the blur of emotions they were creating. The infamous sentence: *"Do this and it will be good exposure for your future in your career!"*.

The truth was that they were trying to delegate a pain of theirs. Like one feeding a kid's ambition & hope for a candy along with what they will miss: *"If you don't, you will miss the opportunity of earning a lollipop!"*.

Taking advantage of a person's ambitions & hopes will have a reverse cycle and pain & fear will take over and become resistant. You see, when we choose to do wrong, life is always waiting to hit back, and it will always be at the worst time. You may get a sale from your client's emotions and then what? Their logic eventually awakes following their purchase and here comes the regrets along with snapping out of their emotionally positive illusion. Remember what you just read because you will realize the impact this may cause with the 1:250 rule. As an Author-Preneur in a world with likely more book titles than there are readers, I can speak about this. Here's an example.

A great idea takes over their thoughts and they decided to take one definite step forward. Yes, one started writing their first book as an Indie Author. Deep inside of them, the big dream of achieving great success with what they will labor hard for. In the emotional illusions with *life & time*, their positive emotions take over along with their ambitions & hopes, and they are hungry for a pineapple! An illusion fed by a niche number of authors who became successful with their work along with earning millions. The illusion of achieving "best seller" as their trophy for a fulfilled life.

That said, several emotional Fishermen are ready to fish for their ambitious emotions. The newly Indie Author is likely not sure about how to complete a successful process. It can feel like a pain, and they are likely not confident right now. What happens? They start to Google, "How to self-publish," and that's what the Fishermen are tracking, and they will ask for at least $5,000 and more for a service that the newly Indie Author can do themselves. Serving as a mindset:

For everything we lack positive curiosity and for everything we are lazy to learn, we allow plenty of people to profit from us.

On top of that, not only are they charging thousands, but rarely the times they will show themselves, meaning that most of their services are by email. The emotional fishermen will share the following excuse: *"it's for security purposes"*. Each time I am approach by a potential fisherman; I ask if we can schedule a virtual camera-on for a greet & meet. Believe it because it's true, 99.9% do not reply to my request. Pause and reflect on this because there are people calling themselves *professional marketers* and asking for a $100,000 one-year service. Is requesting for a camera-on virtual greet & meet fair if one is asking for that amount? It just shows how fishy and likely sloppy their services are. Because the newly Indie Author is experiencing strong positive emotions with their ambitions and hopes, the bridge to the logic is closed, and they do not catch the signals like a fish blindness when they see a hook with food on it.

Daily, I receive at least 5 phone calls by fishermen trying to fish for my emotions using sales promises such as: *"I will promote your books, and I guarantee that you will sell* (for example) *50 copies every month."* This type of fishing style comes from a fisherman ignoring what is The Pineapple Theory because no homework was made and learning about your future clients' products and services along with the competition is highly valued to established credibility. The most valuable and free repellent to these fishermen's promises is, *Pay On Results!*

In life, be nice to everyone because you don't know what people are going through. Be nice to those who likely don't deserve it because they need kindness. With these words of wisdom in mind, when *thinking/ acting/ speaking* like a fisherman may have you try to fish someone who will in return make you lose face and take down your credibility with simple words. Here's a short message series I once had speaking this statement and bear in mind, I am approached at least 5 times a day.

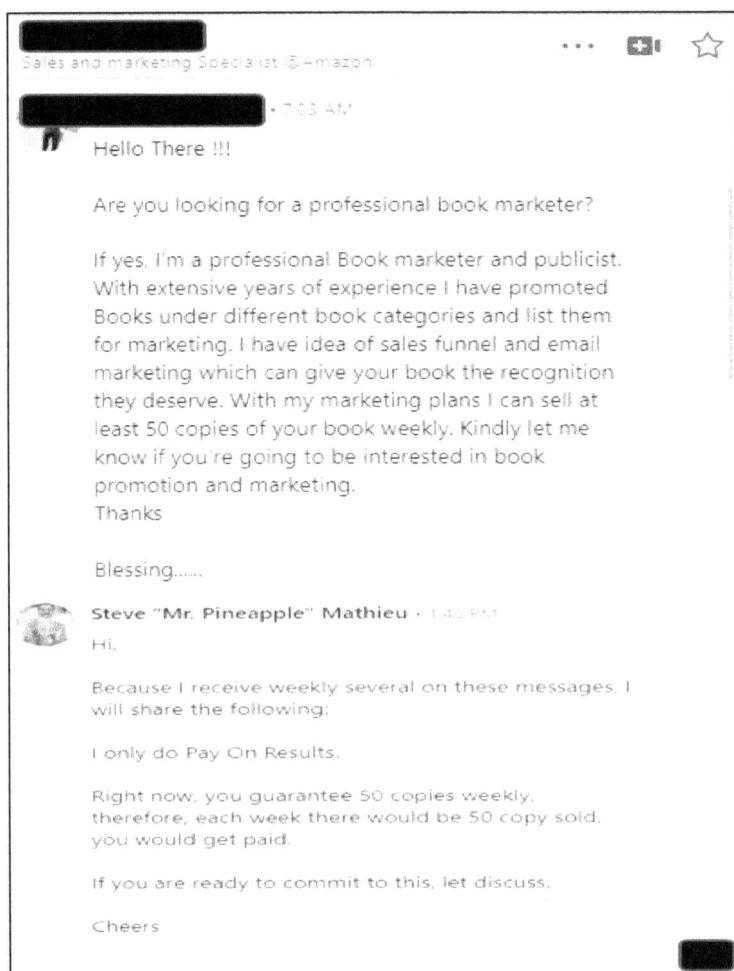

A good salesperson will be a good partner. *Positive curiosity* is a fundamental anchor with the purpose of learning more about one's ambitions and their hopes. Actively listening, meaning listening to understand and not to respond, is a habit. A good partner will share a bit of logic and rational supporting one's ambitions & hopes and burst a few blurs in their emotional illusions with *life & time*. For example: I often browse Facebook's book promotion groups. I completed a survey and discovered that about 90% of the members are Indie Authors, not even book readers, meaning that I am not wasting my time promoting my books. Members wish to sell their work, and they commonly share their pain as follow: *"My book is now available on Amazon KDP since a week and sadly, no sales yet!"* Yes, many, many, and many live with the thought that once they publish their book, that readers will know about them and throw themselves at their book. Sadly, they are blind to brutal reality; there are likely more book titles than book readers and pineapples don't grow with magic beans.

With these promotional groups, I do not only watch, but I also observe their behavior and patterns. As an entrepreneur, consider having multiple revenue streams because there's more than one path to reach the top of the mountain. In my world, each book title is a revenue stream because publishers purchase rights by the title, and it provides more purchase options to future readers.

A few streams will likely be paved from your original product or service. 90% of these promotional groups share ambitions, hopes, and pain. Using the core fundamentals of The Pineapple Theory, I therefore built an Indie Author Mentorship program with the purpose of supporting their ambitions, hopes, and inspiring their bias for action by giving Love – Time – Health. As an entrepreneur and salesperson, I have a product, and I found its niche. From there, all mindsets from this book apply to convert leads to clients by serving a fruitful and welcoming experience, and I do not hide.

Be a farmer.

Make things happen! Next mindset please…

I'm kidding, let me share a few perspectives about this one.

If you wait to be harvested, like living with the thought that everything in life is a miracle, nothing much will happen. In perspective, normality is a paved road and it's comfortable to walk, but no flowers grow. With my creation, what I suggest is, build your own path and be a farmer. You have an idea in mind, deep dive to learn about the process, plant a seed, cultivate it, and discover what grows. Like a scientist, push your *positive curiosity* by initiating studies and research. A problem arises, be a solver, don't dwell on it and don't live it as an excuse on *status quo*. If nothing sweet & fruitful giving Love – Time – Health grows, keep moving, or connect with a mentor to be inspired potential leads to solutions with yourself because it's not about changing your goal, it might be about changing the path to reach your goal.

Working backwards: Earnings from who you are, your products, and services will come from your clients, influenced by you which is harvested from what you have cultivated and planted. Be consistent because it will define your determination, and when educating yourself, also educate your mind and heart.

This may feel like a peculiar analogy but somehow, it speaks truthfully because it's life *Law of Balance* in action when facing a problem, a negative experience with a client, or a failed experiment feels like a pain. The peculiar analogy is that this type of pain is like shit (*poopoo* for our inner child!). Inside what is *shitty,* there's gold because a farmer cultivates the soil with *poopoo* as a fertilizer. In other words, within what is negative, there is something positive. Find it by seeking out because the positive solution is YOU.

About the last analogy, let us never forget that gold from poopoo was the main topic for the movie Ace Ventura 2.

Always learn how to become a better farmer!

The mindset that made you who you became today, if you stop nurturing its growth, will be the mindset holding you back tomorrow. This is important because for every new level of accomplishment you reach, there will be a new level of problems, and it will always require the focus and strength of your mind.

Being a farmer means always improving who you are and becoming a better version of yourself. You are a work in progress with no beginning, and no end. School is one thing, and what I suggest for continuous education is, read books and have a mentor.

Reading books is a topic often shared with my books of The Pineapple Theory. Reading books improves who you are, by yourself, and that's a big step ahead compared to many who don't even try something for themselves. Many will seek excuses instead of seeking results. Worst, how about people who cannot read and wish to have this ability when those who can read, don't. Meaning that one who can read therefore has no advantage. My recommendation is to read 3 books about a single topic by different authors.

Think of a professional sports team; all players are professionals, and reading three books about a single topic is an approach for learning refreshing ways to use fundamental tools.

Reading three books about a single topic, psychologically, supports the integration of new information by making association with new concepts. Because we can't place new concepts free-floating in our brain, reading three books about a single topic helps to successfully integrate new information into our existing network of knowledge.

The new information needs to be attached to an already existing concept with similarities or association. I also suggest following your reading of three books about the same topic, reading the 1st one again because you will understand it differently now that your brain has built multiple nodes of information into your network.

My 3-book recommendation therefore speaks of psychology with *semantic network*, *similarity principle*, and *classical conditioning*. All important aspects of persuasion when you market & sell yourself, product, and services.

Semantic networking is a theoretical model of how knowledge is organized in the human mind, where concepts are represented as nodes connected by links that signify relationships between them, essentially depicting a web of interconnected ideas and meanings stored in our long-term memory. It helps explain how we access and retrieve related information quickly by activating connected concepts through a process called *spreading activation*

To ease the cultivation of new concepts, with The Pineapple Theory books, the pineapple is an analogy & metaphor for what is already existing information to your network (a pineapple fruit) associated with positivity. Voila, like magic! No, I do not do magic shows, but I can inspire myself with my books and speaking, and you also can benefit from using analogies & metaphors because they are a positive and sweet powerful selling approach.

Be a farmer by cultivating new relations.

Later in this book, I will share leads making this section of the book valuable. In life and in your career, you occupy a high-level position requiring connecting with people, meaning that several of the heavy lifting (micro task) require delegation and here's a philosophical perspective about this.

Certain companies expand globally becoming empires while others stay stuck in the same place and it's not because of the economy, nor because of competition. Several entrepreneurs are trapped working in their businesses and not on it. They are masters of their craft but prisoners of their routine. Imagine owning a bakery, but spending your time kneading dough in. The kitchen was never actually designed the strategy for last.

Don't be an operator in your business but be the architect of your empire because if you're not building a business that works without you, you're not building a business at all.

75% of responders shared that to make money, it's about who you know.

- Networking is a must.
- Attending organizations gatherings is a must.
- Attending conferences is a must.
- Attending fairs as an exhibitor or visitor is a must.
- Be where you'll bring the hospitality of a pineapple!

Attending each will take space in your agenda, often held in spread out time in a schedule, they are valuable to meet new people, and you become a farmer by cultivating new relationships because many will harvest a benefit from yourself for your business in the short, and long term. For this, you simply can't spend your time operating, you must build the vision. I will therefore repeat that you are positively the solution for success with this one: H2H.

Through reading this book, anchor the following when cultivating new relations: Egocentric theory, make them shine, *be positively curious,* and establish similarities. Allow me to introduce you to the following:

High-Impact compliment
In psychology, also referred to as genuine and meaningful praise, *high-impact compliment* suggests a positive impact on a person's well-being, motivation, and self-esteem, potentially leading to increased confidence, stronger relationships, and a more positive outlook.

If you want people to see you as incredibly charismatic, here's how to use high-impact compliments, But not the usual, generic ones.

Instead of saying, "you're smart", say, "the way you explain things makes complex ideas sound simple."

Instead of, "your funny," say, "you have a talent for making any situation more fun."

Specific compliments feel more genuine and stick in people's minds because details attached to your compliment triggers a stronger emotional response, it makes people feel truly seen and appreciated which instantly deepens their connection with you.

Don't sell – rather – educate.

It took me about 3 years to break myself with this one and install balance with harmony. When I first launched my books, I was protective of their content, I was trying to sell instead of educating the heart with their content, and I was experiencing financial pressure because I was out of work for several months due to COVID-19. My pain was an emotional blur and a distraction for doing what is right.

Reading again passages from this book, being a salesperson that only tries to sell is often a turn off because many people are experienced with the classic and *cheezy* technics. With our current technological era of Earth timeline, humans' engagement requires trust, love, and how something will benefit them (ego) by giving them with Love – Time – Health by relieving a pain – by saving a fear – and by realistically supporting their ambitions and hopes. Like multiple small clusters of flowers coming together to form the pineapple, it all comes together.

If you do not often post on social media, reconsider and here's why. Posting every day can transform your social media growth and it's referred to in psychology as the *anticipation effect*, and it suggests that our expectations or anticipation of future events can significantly impact our current behavior, emotions, and cognition, often leading to a greater enjoyment of the anticipation itself than the actual experience.

Meaning that when you show up daily, you're training your audience's brain to expect and crave your content. Let's relate about your favorite Netflix show, for example, that excitement you feel before a new episode. It's *dopamine* at work daily and posting creates the same psychological response to your audience. They start checking for your content automatically and their engagement becomes habit, the algorithm notices, and here's the psychology hack. If you mix up your content types while keeping your posting time consistent, this will create what can be referred to as, predictable unpredictability, meaning that they know when you will post, but they won't know what your post will be.

For references purposes, in psychology, *dopamine* suggests a feel-good neurotransmitter involved in the brain's reward system, motivation, and pleasure, influencing behaviors like seeking rewards and potentially leading to addiction when overstimulated.

I've shared lengthy marbling about this but became the farmer of a new behavior because it's a tool. Use social media and your website to educate. The educational mindset will cultivate trust and love, and it's a stage to showcase your notoriety meaning that you are positioning yourself and demonstrating that you are an expert.

The magic of psychology with this educational mindset will feed the *egocentric theory* and trigger a reverse cycle title referred to in psychology as *reciprocal effect,* which is often seen in models like reciprocal determinism or reciprocal effects models, suggests that two or more factors mutually influence each other, creating a dynamic and cyclical relationship where each factor both causes and is caused by the others.

In sum, because your audience (leads) is often given something, it cultivates their instinct to give something back, meaning, return the favor. Humans are truly led by their emotions, and this section of your reading speaks how important it is to work with philosophy, and study psychology. Applying the educational mindset is becoming a voice of value, and speaking of value, I invite you to watch the following video I posted on my Youtube channel. Then, self-reflect about how this message can serve you, your business, and your leadership.

https://youtube.com/shorts/ZbFV_AKgoRg4?feature=share

What gets measure gets managed.

This last mindset is important and powerful because it has the purpose to burst your emotional blurs and encourage you to keep moving. In other words, when delusional, you escape it.

Working with DATA will engage your rational making more efficient emotional decisions because your mind is involved, and I must share, it is not always easy because it may disturb your self-beliefs. One nurturing their own thoughts with what they think *is/should/could* is often seeking for thoughts like theirs, meaning that they are tricking their emotions becoming a blur and an emotional illusion. With my books and when I mentor, I suggest seeking thoughts different from yours with the purpose to self-assess and move smartly and as precisely as possible.

This mindset is that thought speaking without emotions, without attachment to a belief. People with a high position of authority are often not easily moved by emotions meaning that your thoughts speaking without emotions becomes a solution.

Albert Einstein
Thinking you can achieve different results by always doing the same thing is insanity.

Often shared with my books and supporting Einstein's view, is my creation of the following valuable principle: Master File – Journal – Communicate

Achieving selling success with yourself/products/services means that you will try new things and will to take calculated risk. You must track your results leading to take your next steps in the right direction. I strongly recommend that you become a master with how tracking and working with DATA – or - contract someone to remove this heavy lifting. I personally excel in many things and being the creator of my own principle means that I'm available for mentorship. Allow me to share the following story of mine with The Pineapple Theory.

At my third year with my books, my self-confidence with my product had grown a lot and I was ready to push it outside of the organic growth approach. I took a calculated risk by investing with a media exposure. I connected with a newspaper; I completed a greet & meet with a consultant and felt they were not a fisherman. I was presented with 3 offers, and I chose an article insert in a major newspaper along with a 3-months social media impressions push.

I must interrupt the story to share the following. I was shared 3 options, and this speaks the *theoretically three* fundamental anchors from my suggested conclusions with The Pineapple Theory. When marketing and offering service packages, the theory prevents one from slipping into a psychological concept called, *decision paralysis*, and it's the inability to decide out of fear of making the wrong choice or being overwhelmed by too many options.

Later through your reading, my theoretical three will speak volume in branding and color psychology. Back to my *guinea pig* story.

I took a calculated risk because of the following. Daily, I share on LinkedIn and Instagram, at least 3 freshly new harvested posts/inspirations and I apply my *Master File – Journal – Communicate principle*. Meaning that in an excel file, I log every post and track for each, their rate of impressions vs engagement along with additional helpful information to tweet when needed my post approach and break patterns *(pattern disruptor)*.

Following approximately 3 years of DATA collecting along with additional deep dive about this topic, only 1%-3% of viewers will provide a reaction. Brutal right? Even when you set up paid marking with META, the built-in math projection also gives 1%-3%. If you ever read my theory in-full, just wait to discover several interesting findings about this information.

Wait, how about this peculiar observation; when I publish an article, there are more engagement than actual reading of the article meaning that when adding a one-click action, it gives users a pain, so they don't click! I mean, so much hard labor to create tailor inspirations for a handful of emotional recognition. Quoted by Thanos in Marvel's movie The Avengers – Infinity Stones: *"All this effort for a little drop of blood"* Although, let's us remember what Captain America quotes, *"I can do this all day."*

You see, humans follow in the shadow and in silence. They observe until you reach a level of success that fits them because they are impressed or it fits a success they wish to achieve (what's in for them), therefore influencing them to come out and support. Many people have dreams but don't live them. If you achieve a level of their dreams, they will be interested about it because it will be seen as a ladder. A powerful example of this is when I post pictures from my travels and DATA speaks to me because I'm often outside the 3% standard deviation. Because I'm living a dream that they keep as a dream instead of living it, they start to engage with the post because it fits them. This strongly speaks one more time, the *egocentric theory*.

Here's a perspective about Apple's products. 1%-3% of their products users will camp outdoor with the hope of becoming the exclusive first-time users that will inspire everyone else observing in the sidelines.

Apple's 1%-3% is a reality for everyone with a marketing breakdown as followed, and these are approximate rates from a standard deviation:

- 60% of viewers of an ad don't care meaning that 60% of your reach is rubbish! Emotionally, accept this.
- 37%-39% of viewers require persuasion. They are potential clients requiring conversion with a low – medium - or high interest. Prior

mindsets shared in this chapter comes in-play.

- 1%-3% will instinctively purchase and that is also risky because *Schrodinger's Cat* is implied. If they bough emotionally, their feedback will likely be impulsively emotional, demonstrating again why these mindsets are critical because 1%-3% will influence about 40%. Connecting the dots with all the mindsets shared, nearly everybody purchases with their emotions. Rationality is delayed, or to provide a touch of humor, their emotions took a decision when rationality went to the restroom (toilet for my UK friends). It's like people living with great ignorance, wisdom reached them, but they ran faster! One more reason why becoming a salesperson providing a positive experience is valuable.

I will get to the end of my story, but I must share additional information becoming insightful. 1%-3% influencing 40% speaks the 1:250 rule, also known as *Girard's Law of 250*. Here's what this means with the following Trivia question:

Who is the current *Guinness World Record* holder for the most vehicle sold? Now, play in your mind Jeopardy's game show 15-second countdown jingle!

By its short name, the answer is Joe Girard. He's the record holder because in 13-years of career between 1963-1977, he sold 13,000 vehicles for a daily approximate average of 6, at retail price. WoW! Obviously, Girard success made him a motivational speaker, and he wrote a few books. Emotionally speaking, don't you see yourself achieving WoW results like him? From the introduction of this book, he's a representation of "boots on the ground." If you are *positively curious* and choose to apply the 3-book approach shared earlier, here's a lead!

The reason why I'm sharing Girard's record is because he suggested a valuable pattern inspiring him the 1:250 rule. He attended a gathering following the passing of one. When signing the guest book, he observed the pattern that about 250 people signed. Later when completing a greet & meet with someone (importance of attending gatherings), he learned that they organize wedding receptions. Girard was *positively curious,* and he asked how many people on average attended. The answer was 500 (250 each). This coincidence fed the view of a pattern and inspiration meaning that 1 client likely knows, and/or could influence, 250. One more time, this speaks again value about your clients experience along with the H2H.

Today 18 June 2023, something fruitful happened and it inspired this paragraph. I came back from the fitness center (gym) and one member told me they purchased a t-shirt of The Pineapple Theory. It became cleared to whom I fulfilled an order that same morning. The client/gym member told me: *"I can't wait to receive my t-shirt because it looks great. I will speak about it to my daughter who will then speak about it to her friends."* Two thoughts were harvest from their comment:

Uno

One new client is ready to spread the word about The Pineapple Theory with a potential reach of 250. How about this, 11 days later, on 29 June, I received a second order from the same gym member and the t-shirt was a different size. The following day, we attended the gym at the same time, they came towards me and shared: *"I warn my pineapple t-shirt at the restaurant yesterday, it looked awesome, my daughter loved it and asked me to order one for her. Then, the restaurant owner asked me where they can purchase it."*

Deuce

I share in my books that weightlifting is my *daily feel-good* meaning that every gym member could become a client. It demonstrates the importance to be myself because one can't live life being someone else because they will make their life much more challenging. Back to my story.

Following my 3-months investment, I received a DATA report. The consultant is ultimately a salesperson, and they spoke about the DATA like if the results were awesome and above their average results. This is intended to stimulate my emotions because then what? Let's try making me a returning client. The DATA shared spoke the 1%-3% reaction from the social media impressions push. Check on that one. Here's how the remaining rule of this mindset influenced my next step, which made the consultant mouth dropping quiet realizing the powerful reasoning that you will soon discover from the pineapple.

- Was I tracking traffic on my website? Yes
- Have I observed a traffic increase on my website? Yes, about 40%.
- Have I observed an increase of new subscribers to my blog/newsletter? NO
- Were new sales recorded? NO (Brutally painful by the way!)
- Was I a returning client? NO

I was not a returning client because the timing and/or approach was not right. I may have achieved the 1%-3% post engagement from the impressions push but I have not had sales from the 1%-3% of emotional buyers, no 40% of new subscribers (or 1%-3% would also have worked for this scenario), meaning that I cannot meet the 1:250 rule. Therefore, *Schrodinger's Cat* was dead in the box, and the 1%-3% was a smoke show.

Additionally, if I focus on DATA alone, it is me only seeking around and that's no good. How can I positively be the solution? Where is the gold in the *poopoo* situation? When seeking within, also when actively listening to someone speak, pick on the following fundamental anchors of my theory - cue words because you will prevent tricking your emotions. Remember that I have an investigative background, and these words are crucial when seeking accuracy with a purpose from one's Desire-Motive-Opportunity.

What you **think is, should, and could** is not a fact. Be positively curious.

What you **assume, guess, predict** is not a fact. Be positively curious.

Because, if, and buts are roadblocks of self-awareness, they are excuses and not a search for solutions leading to results. Be positively curious.

I'm an Author-Preneur in a world with likely more book titles than there are readers, meaning that I must challenge myself. If this was you in that situation, what do you have control of? *Be positively curious* because there are always positive solutions.

When seeking around, you are pointing to blame. From my books, seek within first because that is what you can control and that's where answers are. I was maybe not a returning client <u>for now</u>, but I did challenge my product with the purpose of improving it. I made my blog & newsletter subscription section more upfront on the main page of my website. This book cover now have a different approach when compared to prior books of The Pineapple Theory. Additionally, if this book cover page works great, already released books cover page – and future books - will require an update for brand consistency because DATA from my experiment will be revealed as positive/positive. These are only a sample of factual examples.

Sometimes, you need to give yourself your own slap to face to wake up and see things differently along with your own ass-kicking to move forward. Again, be the *guinea pig*, be the pineapple in a mixed plate of fruit, and always cultivate a growth.

<u>80/20 - 64/4 – 51/1</u>

Pareto's Law is also known by the name 80/20 rule. Each book of The Pineapple Theory starts with a chapter titled *The Management of Emotions*. If you read that chapter and observe it, I call it Pareto's principle or the 80/20 principle. Personally, I view the 80/20 rule as a principle because for decades, it has proven its value to become a fundamental to spend wisely our emotional energy in life, and business.

Developed by Italian economist Vilfredo Pareto in 1896, Pareto observed that 80% of the land in Italy was owned by only 20% of the population. He also witnessed this happening with plants in his garden meaning that 20% of his plants were bearing 80% of the fruit.

With the purpose of spending smartly your emotional energy to influence 80% of your results, your 20% is valuable and once you have collected enough DATA with the *Master File – Journal – Communicate principle*, the application of the 80/20 principle becomes more efficient and obvious.

To profit more from the 80/20 principle, I enjoy applying the 64/4 rule. I shared earlier the concepts of the 1%-3% of first comers/buyers, the 40% of "maybe", and the 1:250 rule. Allow me to support these concepts with the 64/4 rule.

64% of your revenue will be influenced by 4% of your clients. The same can be applied with your actions in your business and life meaning that 64% of events will be influenced by 4% of action possibilities. The math behind it is the 80/20 principle applied to itself meaning that you compound it. Here's an example that will one more time speak about the importance of working with all the mindsets as one. Coincidentally, it fits again with my *Theoretical Three* fundamental anchor.

You have your basic product or service. The *Theoretical Three* then starts as follows.

- You have an upgrade called Silver and 20% of your clients will happily pay for it.
- You also have another upgrade called Gold and 20% of them – meaning 4% of total clients - will purchase.
- Lastly, you have the Platinum and 20% of 20% of 20%, meaning 1%, will buy.

The 1% from your Platinum offer is the 51/1 rule meaning that you now have the 80/20, 64/4, and 51/1 rules becoming tools to live efficiently by spending wisely your emotional energy and making confident calls (decisions) and supporting earning money with your business. Does this give Love – Time – Health?

Here's a last perspective: If 1% influence 51% of your income, the *Master File – Journal – Communicate principle* will efficiently show you who they are. Focus on them with in mind the 1:250. Understanding that it's about people is crucial as a leader and when being the architect of your products and services. Money is a must because it's like oxygen for your business and living. Without it, you likely suffocate, you need it. Do the right things to earn clean money though, be consistently a farmer and positive results will be harvest by earning one's heart.

Surveyed by The Pineapple Theory

Which would you like more of?

46%: Health
41%: Time
13%: Love

SEED
CULTIVATE
HARVEST

Overview

With the purpose to inspire you leads to solutions by poking at your curiosity, this chapter is an introduction - high-level view – about various topics worthy consideration when thinking of launching a product and service, or they may be used to apply the *sling-shot concept* suggested with The Pineapple Theory, suggesting of stepping-back, rethinking, organizing & structuring your thoughts, and relaunching to go further and faster. What I suggest as a life & leadership philosopher is the calmer you are, the clearer you think meaning, move with strategy, not with emotions. Per a German proverb, think first, then act and per an English proverb, let's go back to the drawing board.

As a farmer, growth continuum means there are consistent changes because the cultivation methods are updated. Creating the seeds, cultivating them, and what you and your clients will harvest is fundamental. What you wish to accomplish with yourself, your products, and services starts here along with a fruitful mindset.

Bear in mind that I do not have leads to solution for everything, I share insights & perspectives, and you must *be positively curious* about other tools. For example, cold calling. I hate it, I don't do it, meaning that I would not be a voice of value about this topic. This does not mean it must be avoided because it truly depends on the type of business you operate. For me to cold call someone with the purpose of selling a book is low, and weird.

A second topic I will not share is how you choose to present yourself, meaning, how you look. Several countries are experiencing an unbalanced change with diversity & inclusion. My view with The Pineapple Theory is that the ultimate purpose is not about difference blindness – rather – it's about a non-conscious acceptance with differences. Psychological studies about how we look and present ourselves share a variety of outcomes which may cause confusion, but several studies share that how we look and present ourselves gives value for ourselves, and others. Though, what I can share is that people purchase their fruits by how they look, then they feel, and their limited DATA gives a judgement meaning whether they will purchase or not. In sum, it's beauty before taste. I know I'm rambling but allow me to share more details about this.

No matter what many may say, appearance and beauty standards does matter in life, and the best example I can share is when people are purchasing fruits. I call it the *psychology of fruit,* and I can make it a philosophy because I'm living the appearance and beauty standards with an appealing and tempting book cover. With my theory, from the patterns with our *emotional timeline,* I suggest the following philosophical thought: Many people invent, critic, and accuse others when they never met them. In perspective, a fruit's appearance is per standard from everything surrounding us since we were a child and it's what makes a fruit look fresh, tasty, and constructing us with a mental picture of enjoying it. The fruit's beauty example has deep roots within humans' psychology explaining the tough challenge major grocery chains had with the attempt to sell and educate their customers with the quality of their "ugly" product line was not inferior. For society, again, it's sadly not taste before beauty - rather - it's beauty before taste.

To piggyback my fruit analogy, every fruit has its authenticity and is accepted the way they are, though, always be self-aware with open eyes and with an open mind about how you present yourself. When I exhibit at bookfairs for example, I adjust what I wear based on the country's culture and if I wish to influence business with a specific country, I will manipulate non-consciously their representative by voluntarily wearing fashion wear commonly with their culture because non-consciously, they will be attracted to approach, then have a feel of me.

Together, we will walk a pineapple plantation of various topics. Pineapples pick that you find the most insightful which would benefit you at making a sweet addition to your exceptional recipe. The philosopher in me wishes to inspire you with several leads to solutions with each mindset previously shared, and every pineapple ingredient and tool you are about to read. This book is like what school is, meaning that you are learning how to think, and not what you should be thinking. Make your reading a success and write key words in a notebook or whiteboard. Write them as if they were categories, connect them, and write your thoughts about how each topic would fit what you do.

Your niche

If you think that somebody will do it, it means that nobody will do it. Applied with the purpose of marketing & selling yourself, your products, and services means that if your target is everyone, it means no one. Emotionally, and will you read this again later, I still fight this a little because The Pineapple Theory's purpose is assisting a more pineHapply living, together, by adding a pineapple to people's life, leadership, and business recipes. Therefore, everybody deserves a more positive living. That said, I also remember that there's more than one path to reach the top of the mountain, meaning each path to achieve a meaning speaks to a niche. This application helps break through resistance from a belief and work towards a solution.

If 1%-3% are leading the way and are the influencer of 40%, and if 1%-3% are leading the way inspiring to apply the 1:250 rule, I need to emotionally re-think that everyone deserves a more positive living. Meaning that, I'm not sharing that they don't deserve it but rather, I'm sharing that I must consider keeping focus on the 1%-3% because if I don't, I will drain my emotional energy with the attempt to convert people who don't care because they don't want to listen to me. But 1 to 250, that's the efficient approach to reach others' attention. What is their niche and why would they purchase from me? An existential philosophic question like *"who am I?"* or *"what is truly living?"* or *"what is time?"*

A close friend of mine and their sibling have been entrepreneurs for several years. They have had their ups & downs throughout their journey, like we all have. The product they focus on truly is an awesome. Even Samsung exhibited it in their home of the future. Their product is called *The Smart Duvet,* and here's how it speaks about finding your niche.

At the palm of your hand with your cell phone, your bed will make itself and there's a bi-zone temperature setting. With only one sentence, what are niches in your mind and how can they be reached? Because their product stands alone, the initiators, meaning the 1%-3%, acted, and spoke. Many claimed that:

- It saves relationships.
- Many enjoyed seeing their bed make itself.
- Many improved their night sleep because the temperature was perfect.

Love – Time – Health; does the *Smart Duvet* checks all boxes with the suggested fundamental anchor? Is the product relieving pain? With this additional DATA about the *Smart Duvet*, does it assist better in defining prospective niches?

Your purpose

This topic of the book could have been the first because everything becomes inspirational when there's a *why,* and I wish to propose you with the following exercise.

With the available DATA, can you write 3 purpose options for the *Smart Duvet?*

Marketing & selling yourself, your products, and services must have a purpose to become your WOW statement. Like a punch line picking people's interest. My tip is by adding a business philosopher to your recipe because it's a non-biased mind that will likely inspire you with alternative perspectives. Here's a brief fun fact about how a business philosopher can speak volume for your seed of thoughts.

A business philosopher is someone who challenges your beliefs and helps you stepping back from your tree – or your problems – so you can see the forest – or the bigger picture. Per my theory, it's referred to as, *the sling shot principle.*

The business philosopher is someone who questions you so you can see opportunities where others see only problems. People who had great successes are often supported by coaches. When Eric Schmidt became CEO of Google in 2001, people around him told him he needed a coach. At first, he was reluctant, saying: *"Why would I need a coach? I'm CEO of Google".* But he was presented with Bill Campbell, the same coach who was working with Steve Jobs.

Your client's Avatar

Once you have established your niche…
- 🍍 Who's your perfect audience?
- 🍍 How do they present themselves?
- 🍍 How do they express themselves?
- 🍍 How do they think?
- 🍍 What can your purpose do for them?

This is a big homework assignment requiring a whiteboard, a philosopher, and additional partners. If you market & sell yourself, your products, and services on LinkedIn for example, your perfect client's Avatar will likely be different from your clients on Instagram, like some countries cultivating different types of pineapples.

Defining your client's Avatar will not be an easy task because there are new generations of humans' lineage on deck and previously shared, the scientist in you must *be positively curious* with new cultivation technics. Allow me to share the following philosophy with the purpose of inspiring a lead of thought:

In life, questions remain the same, but the answers are changing.

Your email list and following.

An email list is precious DATA. It's an audience with an open interest and curiosity in you, your products, and services. Find creative ways to feed your DATA "bank account." Because pineapples don't grow with magic beans, there is this pain requiring patience with marketing when spending to be discovered. When choosing this approach, avoid becoming a *me too*, meaning like everyone else because that's what most do. The reason I define them a *me too* is because many will seek what others do, meaning – *meme theory* in motion, which is an obvious a pattern and reflex to seek for.

In psychology, *meme theory* explains the development of culture through the imitation of things: ideas, behaviors, and styles that are encoded as memes so they can be easily imitated.

From earlier in this book, be a *pattern disruptor*! Be the pineapple standing tall that can't be missed in a variety of fruits. If we apply the 1%-3% of people who impulsively became a client along with an approximate 40% requiring to be influenced to become a client, each can become your sponsor – a voice of value - influencing the 1:250 rule.

The more you keep reading this book, the more you must bridge each section together because they are all connected like all the pages of this book assembly making one book. A fun fact about the last sentence is that it takes multiple clusters of flowers coming together to form one pineapple. Allow me to share a story from one of the several freelance photographers I collaborate with speaking about how topics of this book easily come together.

The photographer has an urban style and chose to take on the streets of London to shoot random people. It is a superb initiative to give a brief experience to people who likely never considered a photoshoot before, and because people can see it to manage it, there's paved roads to eventually reach the photographer for more. My *positive curiosity* with this initiative allowed me to not only recognize the photographer's do-it-yourself and always show up initiative, but I helped suggesting an important missing piece of the puzzle. *"Do you give people a business card to claim a free picture?"*, I asked. The answer was, "no".

Forged the iron while it's warm, meaning, give a card to claim a free picture while their emotions are high, and you'll deposit new contacts in your email list, and they are future leads with whom you can consistently connect with.

Position yourself and build trust.

You are the subject matter expert, showcase it! Though, bear in mind that emotionally, humans are easily intimidated and often can't accept others' brilliant mind and knowledge above average. One more reason why creating your perfect client's Avatar is valuable. Showcase your expertise in a way they will emotionally feel you are like them. Behind this approach, the wisdom from what you show will be felt, and the genius in you will hit a target no one else could see.

Social media is a valuable communication channel to position yourself and establish trust. I must share; content creation takes time and time is a currency. Plan it and find efficient ways to complete this process. If it's overwhelming and you are stretching yourself with this task, consider collaborating with a social media manager. A personal recommendation by applying my suggested *theoretical three* fundamental anchor is, limit yourself to three social media platforms.

Be positively curious and learn about it. Keep your shares short & sweet because time with our technological era is a blur in the emotional illusions with *life & time*. Reels on social media are impactful because not only does the algorithm push to non-followers, but your Reels showcase something ranging from 30-seconds up to 2-minutes requiring a first second impact for interest.

Reflecting on Charlie Chaplin, then it followed Mr. Bean, and more recently LOL, I personally suggest finding a clever way to create Reels without the need to speak, text free, and you will add efficiency along with a worldwide reach with a single short video. With our ongoing technological era of the timeline, the bareness of a busy lifestyle feeds our emotional illusions with *life & time*, and views are impatient when they scroll.

Everything is fast paced; feeling the need to respond to messages ASAP, a product or service is delivered ASAP, why wait one week for your beloved TV show when streaming platforms offer it now, and feeding the emotion that results must be now, ASAP. This view and reality of the generation and theoretically the future ones will likely push the limits of your creativity to lean your messages, make them impactful, in such way time is likely paused for your audience giving you, their attention.

Since I launched The Pineapple Theory, I always share that when people hear me speak, they purchase. That's true with the 80/20 principle. When I exhibit at book fairs for example, I purchase a book inventory with the purpose of selling them, not only to exhibit them. How many must I consider having with me? It's time to become a buyer. I honestly do not wish to carry the pain of travelling back home with an overstock, and the 80/20, 64/4, and 51/1 rule becomes helpful and can be applied as follows:

Annually, on average, how many visitors attend the fair? The 2022 Frankfurt Book Fair (FBM), which was my very first fair for its entire duration, had 180,000 visitors. Here's the math:

- From the 1%-3% rule, I chose 2% = 3,600
- Then, I applied the 51/1 meaning 1% considered "premium" clients = 36 books.
- 36 highly potential "premium" clients with the 1:250 rule = 9,000 potential additional leads to cultivate.

Theoretically, best practice would have been consider starting with 1% of emotional "premium" clients, but I took a calculated risk, and I was ambitious because I bet more on my H2H abilities to push my limits to succeed and give the best value. Also, FBM is a five-day event with 3-day access for the general public. For the 2022 FBM, I sold out.

For each book fair I exhibit, I sell out or have less than a handful overstock. What do I do with the handful of remaining books? I give them to the cleaning staff or to security of the fair because they are often ignored by everyone, and people only interact with them when they need something, meaning the *egocentric theory* is in action. Furthermore, many people in life will act with kindness only to the people they wish to impress or the people that can do something for them. When kindness is part of your soul, you don't feel the need to impress anyone. When I give the remaining handful of pineapple inventory, it is like a welcoming gift making them smile and with a positive emotion that will be remembered. An act making 1 share their experience to 250 more.

Offering

From centuries of awareness suggesting and reminding society at acting with kindness when we wish for a person's kind act for us, the offering is valuable when marketing & selling yourself, your products, and services. Example:

Your support to a not-for-profit and/or support to the community is giving Love – Time – Health to the people experiencing pain, fear, with the need to nurture their ambitions & hopes. Additionally, because they can be viewed as currencies, giving Love-Time-Health with the offering serves – and - is a healthy gesture for your business and personal brand, meaning from your heart to others heart.

Experiences from offering can inspire emotional storytelling for your audience, and it gives visibility to many who don't know about you. Importantly, you are giving back because you care, and it comes from a place of good. It's a seed that you cultivate and yes, something can be harvested.

Copywriting

Crafting persuasive text to motivate an audience to take specific action, such as making a purchase or clicking a link which is a crucial element of marketing and advertising makes copywriting an art, and one mastering this art is a word wizard. One sentence properly written will move approximately 40% of an audience to become positively curious along with 1%-3% emotionally acting.

One inspiring sentence fitting a goal, combining the psychology behind relieving a pain, saving a fear, or supporting people's ambitions & hopes by giving Love – Time – Health as a solution can go a long way. When adding humor and metaphors with an image, it feels like adding boosters to a pineapple to make it fly high. Although I'm an author, I must always seek tips & tricks from books about copywriting, or with freelance simply to discover refreshing approaches or styles giving me a push of new inspiration. I always try to improve my copywriting.

Because I wish to offer you value, I recommend adding the following book to your toolbox, *The Big Book of Words that Sell*, by Robert W. Bly.

Also, following several fails & wins, the following words have proven to be appealing.

- 🍍 To grab attention: Startling, Suddenly, Sensational, Remarkable, Revolutionary.
- 🍍 To launch a product: Offer, Bargain, Introducing, Announcing, Improvement.
- 🍍 To get people to act: Now, Hurry, Quick, Wanted, Challenge.
- 🍍 To spark interest in your ideas: Easy, Magic, Miracle, Amazing, Compare.

Communication

Theoretically and historically, along with many that may have not accepted other's thoughts leading to humans' conflicts, communication is likely an important trigger of conflicts. Allow me to share a story.

Along with my Author-Preneur life, I'm an active professional supporting a corporate company. One morning with the field team, I shared a *good morning* in Arabic with a manager speaking Arabic. Like there are various ways to speak French (my mother language), there are various ways to also speak Arabic.

The manager shared with me how the Arabic *good morning* is pronounced where home is for them. It was slightly different. Coincidentally, two additional managers joined our quick morning chat, and they were also Arabic speakers.

Each was from a different Arabic speaking Country, and each started to share how *good morning* is pronounced. Instantly, a debate ignited with what was the proper Arabic way to pronounce "good morning". I actively observed and listened. Once I got tired of the drama, I interrupted, and asked them:

"In French, there are several words that no matter the Country, they are pronounced the same and have the same meaning. Does Arabic have universal or standardize words like that?"

The 3 managers responded *"no"*.

I asked them: *"How about shkran (thank you)?"*

They realized that yes, *shkran* is one, and then, they were back to their argument about finding common pronounced words, and how words should be pronounced. It truly amazed me to observe their reactions and that is when I voiced a peculiar *pattern disruptor* by sharing:

"See, something as simple as communicating with basic words is likely why with history, war started and still is today. Someone traveled, simply asked if they wish to become friends, and because they could not be understood, it became war!"

They had a good laugh, and we moved forward with our day.

Personalities

What's your future clients' personality? When completing a greet & meet, the *be positively curious* core fundamental anchor from The Pineapple Theory is valuable to quickly determine one's personality. If you are interacting with someone you know a little, or best friends with, you can proactively rehearse conversation leads based on their personality.

Here are four types of personalities with their most common ups & downs. Take quality time to self-reflect. I must share one big exception about these 4 personalities which was previously shared in this book. There are a few high-level decision makers that are completely detached from their emotions. Personally, I hate it and find it cold & challenging, but I do appreciate the straight to the point, DATA driven, they will provide and straight forward response, and they have an amazing view of the big picture because being detached from their emotions is them above the blur of their own and others emotional illusions with *life & time*. Only something to keep in mind.

Dominant (Ups): Determined, decisive, independent.
Dominant (Downs): Lack of empathy, impatience, domineering.

Expressive (Ups): Enthusiastic, creative, communication.
Expressive (Downs): Disorganized, talkative, unfinished work.

Amiable (Ups): Diplomatic, supportive, loyal.
Amiable (Downs): Not assertive, reactive, change resistant.

Analytical (Ups): Thorough, disciplined, structured.
Analytical (Downs): Rigid, unemotional, perfectionist.

Keep it lean.
Have you ever experienced the following:

You: *"Hi, good to see you, how are you?"*
Responder: They respond their life story!

Giving your future client to much information when it was not asked will – theoretically - quickly have them disengage and their nonverbal will express it. Eye contact becomes a challenge, they consistently look around like searching for an escape path, or they look at the time making them realised they are wasting it, or they feel like time paused! Personally, my tip is keeping your communication lean and simple. Also, don't just see, observe, meaning that you must pay close attention to your audience non-verbal and quickly adapt your speaking to pique their interest.

Inspired from several interviews I have completed in my ongoing career for people's dishonest behaviour, not limited to, here are valuable non-verbal to observe.

🍍 People crossing legs as soon as they sit tend to have strong ambitions and proactive attitudes.

- People touching their chins while speaking are generally cautions in their actions. That's often me!
- People often and suddenly crossing their arms over their chest usually have strong opinion and can also be quite stubborn.
- Beware of people looking surprised for more than three seconds, it's often fake.
- When people mirror your body language often means the conversation is going well.
- People laughing too much, even at the stupidest things, often feel deeply lonely within.
- When people's voice goes up & down, it often exhibits an interest.

Lean
Copywriting is valuable for this, along with an every day deeper knowledge about yourself, your products, and services because you are the subject matter expert. Albert Einstein shared that when you understand something, you can explain it simply.

To piggyback Einstein's quotation, what I suggest is don't just know, understand, *be positively curious* and always be a student. Even myself I'm challenge with lean written communication because English is not my native language, and I often write like I speak. Also, I refuse to use A.I. when writing because I wish to serve an organic product, human made, from my soul to yours, and not the one of a machine.

A.I. would be the easy road and what is easy often leads no where, meaning that you don't truly grow. Therefore, I choose the more difficult road making me grow and become stronger. Psychologically, humans will nearly always take the easy road meaning that they exert less mental effort. Human's laziness is by nature, and it's another fundamental anchor of my theory because the motivation to produce accurate judgements exist and sadly, those judgements are made using the least amount of effort possible. It is something to bear in mind.

Simple
Emotionally, if your future client is confused and/or have doubts, you will lose a sale, lose a client, and potentially lose 250 new leads.

With 25+ years of leadership experience with boots on the ground, my creative mind as an Author-Preneur had me initiate several training & coaching tools for the team and business partners. These tools are a must because they remove several ambiguities, they hold people's hand when completing a process map and building them is an investment removing several of the heavy lifting coaching often requires. I suggest to not delay this task. To speak of a pineapple analogy, don't properly educate the team about what they are selling, and they will offer pineapples without the crown, like at the following grocery store nearby my home.

Before booking a meeting to present my recommendation, I was testing each training & coaching tool with someone who did not work for the company. Without specific guidance, if they could complete a process by their own, the failure rate inside the business was greatly reduced meaning that confusion and doubt had a low level of risk.

I find Facebook Marketplace to be like a training room. If your ad can influence a quick sale without question, and you receive a 5-star rating, you have done remarkable. A friendly reminder though; there is no perfection in life and do expect exceptions from what I suggest as, *outside the common-sense standard deviation*! Sadly, a large portion of society read to see and not to observe, and common sense is not a gift – rather – it feels like a sentence when many *think/act/speak* like if they have none. Here's an example:

Ad
Available only Saturday 1 June 2023 from 1300hrs to 1700hrs, located at 555 Pineapple Garden, I will be selling freshly harvested pineapples for only $3 each. If you have additional questions, please call 555-555-5555.

Comments
- Comment 1: I love pineapples, how much are they?
- Comment 2: What is the latest I can get one? I need to know the cutoff, please advise.
- Comment 3: Love it, how can I order one?
- Comment 4: Would you take $2?
- Comment 5: I sent several messages and I'm not receiving a response. Can anyone respond back because I really want a pineapple.

It is said that the customer is always right. Instead, what if the right customer is always right? The philosophy I wish to share is choosing the right clients will greatly serve you with Love – Time – Health because the wrong client will drain your emotional energy and its often-bad soil. Why - What – Where – When – Who – How are called the 5W's, and if your lean message responds to the 5W's and there are people draining your emotionally energy because they *see* instead of *observing*, you likely have a choice to make. The right customer will often share with you the right feedback, the one pushing you to reflect with the purpose to keep growing. When I write that they will share feedback, it does mean that they will literally express one per say, what I'm sharing is that many will share a question or act in a way requiring you to be an active listener and observer to question yourself about how you can improve. This is only true is you seek within before seeking around.

Be consistent and kind even if one is not the right customer because of the 1:250 rule. Example from my first book fair, everyone asked, *"what is The Pineapple Theory?"* and my short response to the first handful of people had them respond: *"I don't quite understand."* Seeking around in my mind would be *"what is it you don't understand?"* But seeking within is acknowledging the signals from an active listening to understand, meaning that the short response required a quick fix.

Lean and simple is also viewed as avoiding sending a 40-page document speaking your products or services. In perspective when selling yourself for job opening, do you submit a 40-page resume or a lean and simple 1-2 pager?

I support corporate companies since the last 25+ years and if what you wish to share is not a 1-pager, their interest is lost. Here's a perspective with the following scenario. Let's say that you meet someone offering their products, but you need to run because you have a commitment. The discussion was promptly interrupted, and you are told: *"I'll send you an email with the details, let's connect once you completed the review."* Boom, a 40-page document is sent. It's heavy, especially when living in our current era of the timeline for which many lack time to share a *"thank you"* to someone.

This scenario speaks what I shared at the beginning of this topic, it has the purpose to give Love – Time – Health, and it simply share what you understand. If your future client wishes to discover more, you will know. If you don't hear back, a clever follow up message does the trick. Anyone who worked with me likely once received the following, often sent 1 or 2 days before the start of the weekend because their emotions experience an emotional incline, and I benefit from this motion. Here's a generic example:

"Hi (or hello, or greetings)

I hope this week is treating your great and awesome plans are on deck for this weekend.

I wish making sure my previous email safely reached your inbox.

Cheers,"

Before moving on with Color Psychology, remember that when marketing & selling yourself, products, and services isn't just what you say, it's how you say it and cultivating small word changes when communicating means you can harvest big impact. Let's glance at the following topic which part of it can also be voiced.

Written communication
The type of fonts to use must be considered because they will influence your audience feelings. Remember that humans are not only feeling their emotions, but they also built them which is known by marketers, and they will become the architects of humans' emotions. Here are examples worthy consideration with your *positive curiosity* if you wish your products and services to convey.

Fonts
🍓   Serif (or Sherif) fonts are known to convey trust, respect, and authority.

Used by AirBnB, Dior, and Pinterest for example.
- San-Serif fonts convey honesty, progressiveness, and sensibility. Used by Amazon, Google, Jeep.
- Script fonts represent elegance, fun, and creativity. Used by Cartier, Hallmark, Kellogg's

Word swaps
Referred to in psychology as *framing*, it suggests that how information is presented, or framed, significantly influences how people perceive, evaluate, and make decisions, even if the underlying information remains the same. Meaning that by presenting this small addition in a way that aligns with the person's current worldview, you reduce the likelihood of resistance. The brain is more likely to integrate information that feels congruent with what it already believes, even if the new idea is subtly different.

Words matter; they influence at making you become more desirable and valuable. This important principle will change your perspective forever about how you market & sell yourself, products, and services because it pushes you to always better understand your audience and *frame* your communication accordingly. Essentially, the message is the same, but the impact is completely different framing, and it eliminates the negatives by highlighting the positives which is the essence of The Pineapple Theory. Simple tweaks can transform how your audience sees you, your products, and services. Not limited to, here are word swaps samples floating in mind as I'm writing this:

Single word
- Act → Here's how this will benefit.
- Affordable → Worth every penny.
- Best → Top-rated
- Best deal → smart investment
- Cheap → Affordable
- Discount → Limited time offer or early supported pricing.
- Expensive → Premium
- Features → Benefits
- Few → Limited
- Free → Complimentary or included for you.
- Innovative say → Created for your needs.
- New → Revolutionary.
- Sale → Your advantage
- Special offer → Exclusive access
- Sign up → Join the movement
- Trending → Leading the pack
- Unique → Exceptional

Word grouping
- 🍓 Act now → Spots are filling.
- 🍓 After you sign the contract → after we finalized the agreement
- 🍓 As soon as you pay → As soon as you put down the deposit
- 🍓 Best in the business → Here's what sets us apart.
- 🍓 Buy Now → 3 units left (Loss Aversion under pressure)
- 🍓 Can you pay more? → What budget are you comfortable working with?
- 🍓 Do you want to pay with your credit card? → What form of payment works best for you?
- 🍓 Hurry before it's too late → Smart buyers are getting it.
- 🍓 I can start when you pay us → We can get started once initial retainer is secured.
- 🍓 I'll do it cheaper → I can adjust the scope to your budget.
- 🍓 If you don't have enough, we can't work together → If it's not your priority now, we can revisit it once you're ready.
- 🍓 Limited time only → Before it's gone.
- 🍓 No obligation → Try it, love it.
- 🍓 Risk free → Test it yourself.
- 🍓 Sign up now → Let's get started.
- 🍓 This is our most expensive package → This is the premium option for you.
- 🍓 Trust me → Here's what others have experienced. (Social proof)
- 🍓 We don't do discounts → We offer premium service at the set rate.
- 🍓 We don't negotiate → Our price reflects the quality and results we deliver.
- 🍓 You have to sign the contract → We'll just finalize the agreement.
- 🍓 You need this → Here's how this can help you.

Color psychology

I find this topic valuable because you will use colors to market yourself, your products, and services with images & pictures, videos, press releases, website, and more. Colors speak and can awaken your future clients' emotions, and I must share, luxury brands are artist with this. Here's highlights about this statement.

Primary colors
Not limited to; Lego, Burger King, Mc Donalds, Best Buy, and Ikea use Blue, Red, Yellow which are neon and primary colors for their logo which relate to cheaper products and discounts.

<u>Luxury color</u>
They'll create a sense of exclusivity, premium, and there are several combinations at your disposal. Because patterns can't be ignored, if you carefully observe, seek patterns with known luxury brands but never forget to research for potential new trends. For example, unconventional product names are used to build emotions such as Obsidian shadow or Onyx because creative names add exclusivity and intrigue. Premium color combinations such as Deep Navy/Gold, Emerald/Gold with Champagne, Matte Black/Silver are color pairing instantly elevating people's perceptions.

For example, about color combinations, with this book's cover page, I combined Green and Yellow to convey an affordable wealth and vitality.

My must-read title, The Pineapple Theory's cover page is Purple & White suggesting exclusive and enigmatic.

Although, originally, all my book covers were not designed with in mind luxury, they were designed based on the color matrix at page 49.

Also, and built on my suggested *Theoretical three* fundamental anchor with my theory, color psychology for a logo suggest the 60%-30%-10% rule because it avoids overwhelming your audience, and it's defined as follows:

🍍   60% for primary color.
🍍   30% for secondary color.
🍍   10% is for accent color.

If you have picture or video projects on deck, close-up product such as zoom in on textures, stitching, and fabric details are valuable to elevate because luxury fashion brands highlight craftsmanship to justify premium pricing. Similarly, with someone looking down because it creates a sense of looking up to your product. Before moving forward with my travel research project for my books, I completed a photoshoot trial at home, and the following picture speaks volume about the viewer looking up at me.

2021 pilot – Copyright Steve "Mr. Pineapple" Mathieu - Picture by Anthony "with a camera" Scrocco

For some cultures, a few colors will have a unique meaning requiring you to push your *positive curiosity* because if you don't and wish to exhibit yourself, your products, and services, using the wrong color will be roadblock. There are studies suggesting that about 90% of the time, a snap judgement is influenced by a color alone. One 2020 study that surveyed the emotional associations of 4,598 people from 30 different countries found that people commonly associate certain colors with specific emotions. The study's researchers suggested that such results indicate that color-emotion associations appear to have universal qualities. These shared meanings may play an essential role in aiding communication. According to the study results:

Red: 68% associated red with love.
Yellow: 52% felt that yellow means joy.
Black: 51% of respondents associated black with sadness.
Pink: 50% linked pink with love.
Orange: 44% associated orange with joy.
White: 43% of people associate white with relief.
Green: 39% linked green to contentment.
Brown: 36% linked brown to disgust.
Blue: 35% linked blue to feelings of relief.
Purple: 25% reported they associated purple with pleasure.

(Source: Jonauskaite D, Abu-Akel A, Dael N, et al. Universal patterns in color-emotion associations are further shaped by linguistic and geographic proximity. Psychol Sci. 2020;31(10):1245-1260. doi:10.1177/0956797620948810)

The study is about color psychology and when I wrote this section of the book, I researched color psychology, and I detected colorful emotional patterns with the following popular colors. I have assembled the following table for you with 3 categories to simplify the big picture. I hope this summary will serve you well, and remember to always research because of the following thought of wisdom previously shared

Questions remain the same but with time, answers are changing.

	Emotion	Industry	Used to
Red	Excitement Energy Passion Attention	Entertainment Food Sport Fire protection Children products	Stimulate Create urgency Draw attention Caution Encourage
Orange	Optimistic Independent Adventurous Creativity Fun	Art Entertainment Food Sports Transportation	Stimulate Fun communication Draw attention Express freedom Fascinate
Yellow	Enthusiasm Opportunity Spontanity Happiness Positivity	Food Sports Transportation Travel Leisure	Stimulate Encourage relaxation Awake awareness Energize Affect mood
Forest Green	Safety Harmony Stability Reliability Balance	Environment Banking Real Estate Farming Non profit	Relax Balance Revitalize Encourage Possess
Black	Power Control Authority Disciline Elegance (luxury)	Mosly used in combination with other colors and create contrast.	Hide feelings Intimidate Create fear Mystery
Royal Blue	Thrust Responsibility Honesty Loyalty	Security Finance Technology Health care	Reduce stress Create calmness Relax Secure

<u>Be honest.</u>
When I exhibit at book fairs, I meet a *positively curious* audience, and I share the following:

*"Do you agree that life is positive & negative forces? (*They always respond Yes) *Understanding this about life makes us positively the solution when facing challenging days because life will always challenge us, no matter our high level of positive thinking because there is no perfection in life. Understanding this along with a positive mindset also means that one bad day is not one bad life and no one around us should emotionally pay the price for it. Hurt people don't have to hurt people."*

What can we harvest from this?
I am not trying to feed my future clients with an emotional illusion with a blur of promises about my books (products) being the ultimate solution to always becoming positive in life, all the time. No, the reality is that it is not perfect. Let's not hide or deny it, life can be brutal because it's always testing us, but my books provide philosophy, positive mindsets, tools, concepts, and much more that when practiced, they serve to seek within first, better self-assess to find the positive from the negative, understanding better their own challenges, and removing their own roadblocks.

You see, many think they know more about themselves, their feelings, and reactions than they actually do. It's simply an honest share, and with my years of corporate experience, years as an Author-Preneur, and as a mentor, more and more people wish for honesty. It establishes trust and the *"art of how we approach it"* is truly everything. Setting expectations with honesty is a sweet combo and here's why:

Expectations are powerful and lie in anchoring. When you purchased this book, it was impossible for you to factually know how bad, good, or both it would be. So, you have likely developed a range of expectations. What were the anchors influencing your range of expectations you say? On the back page of this book, you can read the following:

"(..) making you a better version of yourself, a more engaging leader, and a more thriving salesperson."

What if your purchase was influenced by a friend's feedback? How about the star rating on Amazon? In sum, a natural tendency to seek information to confirm your beliefs or expectations are molded because of a psychological concept referred to as *confirmation bias at work,* and it suggests that an employee or manager tends to actively seek out information that supports their existing beliefs or opinions, while ignoring or downplaying evidence that contradicts them, potentially leading to flawed decision-making and a limited perspective on issues within the workplace.

Honesty implies preventing a backfire with the expectation because of a psychological concept referred to as, *expectation spectrum*, and it suggests that expectations, which are beliefs about the likelihood of future events, significantly influence our perception, affect, cognition, and behavior, and can range from basic perceptual and motor functions to complex, sometimes stereotypical beliefs.

It's like a range, and if the expectation or the *anchoring* is too extreme like what is a standard deviation per the Lean Six Sigma Methodology, it will produce a contrast effect and worsen your opinion. Remember that humans feel a strong desire to confirm their expectations because it feels upsetting when information disconfirms their expectations. Keep it honest and realistic. Again, and always, per a philosophy of The Pineapple Theory:

Be Kind and Truthful and life will be Fruitful.

<u>The promise or guarantee</u>
Which of the following relates with you…

Walk the talk?
Don't just say it, show me the contract (or agreement)?
Work your plan?

No matter your answer, if you communicate a promise or a guarantee, you better make sure you are committing no matter if the first "claim" makes you realize there's a loophole. Do commit or it may negatively influence 250 people for each claim. For example, allow me to extrapolate the following rundown.

The promise
"If this book does not inspire you a single insight or lead to solution with the power of the pineapple, what will?"

There's a Canadian Bookstore with a "if you don't like your reading, we will refund you" program, and it only applies to books recommended by the Chief Book Reader Officer. As I'm writing this section, I still do not know if I will move forward with something never done before with Indie books, meaning, if absolutely nothing positively inspires you from your reading, I will refund your purchase.

Here's a generic theoretical math with concepts shared earlier and by applying the Lean Sig Sigma Methodology:

- Let's assume each book is sold for $100.
- Let's assume I sold 10,000 copies (buyers) for a total of $100,000.
- 1% of 10,000 = 100 DPMO (Defect Per Million Opportunities)
- 100 "defects" at $100 each for every 1,000,000 sold = $100,000,000 (sales for 1 million) - $10,000 (from defects) = $99,990,000 remaining in sales.
- Let's assume the margin is 50%. You have a profit of $49,995,000! That's oxygen. Can you breathe with $49,995,000?

From the 1%-3% of emotional buyers, this ratio also becomes a potential standard deviation serving as a reminder that there is no perfection in life and do expect exceptions from a view referred to earlier as, *outside the common-sense standard deviation*. I've shared a generic & extrapolate theoretical math for you to understand the following: Commit, because in life, behaviors never lie.

One "defect" from time to time is expected, even if the claim is a false/positive meaning that one who claimed was in fact positively inspired from the book. Always seek within and prior to launching such a commitment, properly define your program with procedures.

My background in the field of Loss Prevention becomes handy to support with this. For example, with my theoretical book promise, if a reader wishes to claim a refund, the condition will be to schedule a virtual camera-on discussion because I wish to *be positively curious* and always improve my product. Also, show me your proof of purchase. What if as an extra condition, the reader must be a subscribed member to my blog & newsletter? How about this, what if the claim process was only available on the last page of the book to truly confirm they'd read it? Meaning that if they purchased and claimed, then share they did were unaware about the process, they will lose face on their own.

Self-reflect about this section and apply it to any type of promise or guarantee you express in life. Never forget the emotional experience one will remember you for. Building trust like embarking on a voyage. Never create doubt with that trust because it's like playing the board game *ladders & chutes*. The ladder is defined as is installing trust, and the chutes is your fast track down.

Keep selling after the sale.

Inspired by my reading of Joe Girard's book, when my clients have purchased direct from my website, I have their information that I protect and safeguard close to my heart. In 2023, I started sending them a bi-annual surprise letter sent by regular mail. Every envelope sent is individually prepared and handwritten, nicely packaged, and with a content making them smile. It is an operational cost, I have a monthly tracker about this initiative, and it gives a sweet post purchase experience. Must I share that with our technological era, handwritten notes speak volume and can be viewed as "old money".

A happy client is a returning client. What is the likelihood for my clients, recipients of obvious care and focus, will they share it with approximately 250 people? Furthermore, of all the books you have read in your life, how many authors took that one step forward to provide you with personal attention? That's what makes me different, like a pineapple standing tall in a mixed plate of fruit. Ask yourself what type of post-sale experience can you provide your clients with?

Old methods still work amazingly when approached and adapted with our current era. Often suggested with my theory when speaking Earth timeline; *what was still is.* Build the future but learn about the past first.

Your competition is an asset.

One more time, you are the subject matter expect. If you apply the mindsets and various tools from this book, it becomes an asset to know about your competition. I am not talking about their deep secrets, what I mean is what are their products and services ups & downs, and how can you compare with yours?

Maybe you have common ups & downs and will realize that what will make you more attractive is your value. Plant honesty to harvest trust. About value, here's my view but first, allow me to speak about persuasion.

Persuasion isn't about pushing. It's about guiding people to your side without them even realizing it. Reflecting about the 15 fundamental anchors of my theory, I suggest that often, a person will only accept what is accepted when it's from their own self-realization and conclusions. Persuasion is, in perspective, helping them at promptly achieving their self-realization because when you market & sell yourself, products, services, you hope for your audience to say, "yes" to you. Here are 3 phrases and/or questions which you may use most often.

What would it take for you to agree to this?
Instead of arguing, this forces the other person to think about conditions where they would say, "yes."

Most people in your position would
This uses *social proof* to make your suggestion feel like the natural choice. For example, most leaders in your role prefer this approach because it saves time. In psychology, *social proof* suggests that people often copy the actions and opinions of others, especially when unsure of the "right" way to behave, as they assume others possess more knowledge or insight about a situation.

I wouldn't want you to miss out on this.
This persuasive approach creates urgency without pressure. For example, I wouldn't want you to miss out on this opportunity while it's still available.

Many future clients may try to negotiate with you, your products, and services for a discounted price. Don't discount – rather – add value. Shared early in this book, don't try to sell the product, sell the story, and the word swap section from earlier serves insights to counter a discount request.

In perspective, leave the discount business to the big discounters out there, meaning, if you start playing the game of being the lowest price out there, you will find it brutal. Don't waste your emotional energy on this. Add value, be creative, and remember about the post purchase experience. Let me show you one road to consider exploring.

You may have a client that will tell you: *"Yeah, but company "BOOBOO" is cheaper."*

Now, what if your value was the following:
"I agree that "BOOBOO" is cheaper but here's the value I offer you. My products/services will remove you from several pain because you get everything with one payment. "BOOBOO" offers you less and then, you realized that you must purchase extras. Example: If you would like a one-week beach vacation, you could purchase a cheap flight. Then, they will try to sell you a stay at the hotel, and then additional costs will come in play like travel insurance. I am offering you an all-inclusive peace of mind experience."

The above example shares valuable key words. Words like *interested, buying,* and *selling* are often repulsive for your future client and in the example, I used similar words referencing company *"booboo"*. Appealing words like one attracted to a pineapple are often *saved, valuable, useful.* Do you remember what was shared on page 9 of this book?

"Bear in mind that people respond more positively when they are shared what they will lose or miss out on rather than what they stand to gain."

Make them shine!

If you wish to shine like a star, care about making others shine like stars.

It starts with you because it's not about you, meaning that every milestone and success story with yourself, your products, and/or services is not about you. Celebrate within but do it for your clients, make them shine, make them the real heroes and give them recognition. Making your clients the stars will feed the *egocentric theory,* and it will give them Love-Time-Health. Do you agree this approach fits with the 1%-3% of emotional first clients influencing approximately 40% along with the 1:250 rule?

You labored hard behind the scenes, and you are paving the roads – still – it's all about your clients. Your success is their success, and if you have a team, celebrate your team equally, and more is even better. How can you shine by making others shine? There is always a leader behind a team's success, meaning that leaders must provide recognition. Surveyed by The Pineapple Theory:

How does it make you feel when you consistently labor hard and are not provided any sign of recognition from time-to-time? Top 2 answers were: 50%: I feel less engaged and 15%: I quit.

The top 2 answers of the survey will likely become the outcome of your clients about yourself, products, and services. Therefore, I highly recommend making them shine, and you will shine. It is another example of what you can harvest from what you have planted.

Planting the seed of recognition for your clients or team in the workplace is valuable and is referred to as in psychology, *classical conditioning.* Allow me to push this further speaking my careful observation with more than tens of thousands of years with our timeline to identify emotional patterns. People completing a good deed expect a reward. That's how morality was conditioned with human primitives. Also, it strongly speaks of Pavlov's conditioning, a fundamental anchor about humans and life with my theory.

Classical conditioning must be understood and the study behind is as follows, and please, word of cautious; use each persuasion technique from a place of good because it's powerful.

Accidentally discovered like several scientific breakthroughs, Ivan Petrovich Pavlov (1849–1936) was a physiologist, not a psychologist.

During the 1890s, Pavlov researched salivation in dogs in response to being fed. To measure saliva when the dogs were fed, he inserted a small test tube into the cheek of each dog. Pavlov predicted the dogs would salivate in response to the food in front of them, but he noticed that his dogs would begin to salivate whenever they heard the footsteps of their assistant, who was bringing them the food. He later discovered that any object or event which the dogs learned to associate with food would trigger the same response.

The psychology research by Pavlov started from the idea that there are some things that a dog does not need to learn. For example, dogs don't learn to salivate whenever they see food. This reflex is hard-wired into the dog meaning that food is an unconditioned stimulus, and salivation is an unconditioned response.

Pavlov used a metronome (a bell) as his neutral stimulus. By itself, the metronome did not elicit a response from the dogs. The conditioning procedure then began whereby the clicking metronome was introduced just before he gave food to his dogs. After several repeats of this procedure, he presented the metronome on its own.

The outcome is that the dogs had learned an association between the metronome and the food, and a new behavior had been learned. Because this response was learned - or conditioned - it is called a *conditioned response* also known as a *Pavlovian response*. The neutral stimulus has become a conditioned stimulus.

Classical conditioning is important because it surrounds us all the time and that is, since as long as one accepts to see it from our timeline.

Leverage

Villains in action movies love leverage, but for the wrong reasons. They will do whatever they can to track people's lives with the purpose of collecting as much information as possible that would make them lose face, lose their reputation and status, and feel ashamed. For the villains, it's value and currency to negotiate what they want. It's desire for power hiding the motivation to harm.

Because you are a good person, the valuable strategy at making yourself, your products, and services will shine from your milestones for upcoming leverage opportunities. A powerful example, and story, about making usage of your milestones a leverage for yourself, products, and services is recorded as a

Guinness World Record. This will not make me feel younger because I was a young adult thinking it knew everything when it happened because the media started following this story. The story sparked in my mind when writing this section and following my research, I forgot the record holder's home is the same as mine, meaning, Montreal!

Officialized a World Guinness Record in 2007 as the best online trade, Kyle Macdonald initiated on 11 July 2005, a series of online trades starting with a red paperclip and nearly one year later on, 12 July 2006, with the final trade with what is today called The Red Paperclip House. Macdonald' journey with his red paperclip was as follow:

- The first trade was the red paperclip for a fish-shaped pen.
- The pen for a unique doorknob.
- The doorknob for a camp stove.
- The camp stove swapped for a generator.
- The generator was traded for a keg party.
- The keg party for a snowmobile.
- The snowmobiling for an adventure to Yahk, BC.
- Yahk's adventure for a cube van.
- The cube van for a recording contract.
- The recording contract for a one-year condo rental in Phoenix, AZ.
- The one-year condo rental for a day with Alice Cooper.
- Next, Macdonald arranged for a double switch with Actor-Director Corbin Bernsen, an avid collector who agreed to accept a "KISS" snow globe in exchange for a role in an upcoming Hollywood movie.
- Lastly, Kipling trade a house for the role in an upcoming Hollywood movie.

Following a series of a successful trades, Macdonald achieved his goal of earning a house from a red paperclip by consistently leveraging each milestone, and the Kipling leverage the trade resulting the following:

- ✓ Their town has been showcased internationally in the media.
- ✓ Kipling has appeared in many magazines and the 2007 "Ripley's Believe It or Not".
- ✓ The Town of Kipling has also received its certificate from Guinness for building the World's Largest Paper Clip, which stands in their Bell Park, standing tall at 15'2" and weights 3,043 lbs.
- ✓ They had a commercial for Volkswagen in Spain filmed in their town.
- ✓ Kipling and "the trade" have been featured on internet spots such as "What Makes Canada Cool" (www.canadacool.com)

✓ They frequently have tourists stop to take photos in front of the "Paper Clip House" and at the big paperclip in Bell Park.
✓ Trade has resulted in at least four movie-related boosts to their town.
✓ Kipling Film Productions Inc. was formed to finance "Rust" and is being kept alive with a view to producing more movies in the town and district.

The red paperclip trade story is amazing and strongly says that through your journey with yourself, products, and services, use every milestone as a headline and steppingstone to your next desired accomplishment, towards your goal. Sometimes, you may reach accomplishments that were not in-mind because often in life, breakthroughs happen when we are not expecting them like what you seek is seeking you.

For example, I wrote my books in English even if it's not my native language because English is internationally the business language. On that note, I hope your eyes are not bleeding because it's not perfect English but, it is as advertise at the beginning of this book. In fact, and mentioned earlier, French is my native language and one of many objectives was to have my books translated in French. Turns out the first translation for my titles was Arabic, then followed Deutch (German). Still, the milestone of a first translation is now recognition for the publisher, and a foot in the door for leverage.

Every milestone cultivates even better stories. *Journal* them along with their process in your *Master File* because they become great stories for your audience, meaning *Communicate*. Everything starts with one foot in the door serving as a first step forward. Once inside, limitless opportunities can be discovered because imagination takes you everywhere. One definite step forward will lead you to thousands of steps forward.

Lastly, what if you could shine by making your products and services shine?

The red paperclip trade story made the red paperclip shine because it was not only about the paperclip, but it's also the story about the paperclip that made it valuable. It is an example of how to make a product shine and notice it like a pineapple standing exceptionally tall in a mixed plate of fruits.

The tooth fairy!

If losing a tooth when a child earned you money when sleeping, what if you could earn revenue when sleeping possible as an adult? Do you remember the emotion you felt when waking up and feeling excited looking under your pillow? Imagine if you could have that similar feeling when you wake up and browse your products and services back office or sales dashboard. Rich people don't truly work for their money because in fact, money works for them. Now, how can this perspective be applied to you?

Earning revenue when sleeping is a benefit of an online business because it has a worldwide reach. Your creativity will be required along with completing a few research to find solutions best fitting what you do. What if the following could inspire you with leads to solutions?

What if you could subscribe to Amazon's Influencer or Affiliate program? Your social media posting will run worldwide 24/7 with your special web links. That is earning revenue when sleeping. On my end, I leveraged this program with most freelance photographers I collaborated with. Because I often promote them on social media, and because their work can be admired with my books, I produce them a business card with on one-side their information and on the other, one focus title of mine with a QR code meaning, their Amazon Affiliate. Even when I network, if I talk with someone from the UK asking me how they can purchase my books, I share with them the local photographer's Affiliate link. Everybody wins with the collaborative approach.

What if you could make your clients and products shine by creating an Affiliate program, or a Referral program? With this approach, you are removing heavy lifting because you are giving Love – Time – Health and earning revenue when sleeping. The 1:250 rule has leverage because 1 now has an incentive to influence 250+. Loyalty cards are "old money" but still work amazingly great.

One more time, social media is a worldwide 24/7 reach, and new potential clients are purchasing (1%-3%) and following (approximately 40% reach but expect more 1%-3%). Along with this, you also can activate social media Ads, it is a calculated risk, and I propose to contract a freelancer. There are many available on fiverr.com. Please use this QR if choosing a freelancer on Fiverr:

VALUABLE LIKE A PINEAPPLE

What if people could Thrive more pineHapply by adding a pineapple to their life, leadership, and business recipes?

That's my crazy ambitious motivation when I step out of bed because in life, we must always navigate our boat of life with more than one anchor. You see, life is simple, but humans make it complicated because of how they choose to feel & think. Humans' emotions are built, not just felt, and I have embarked the grand *guinea pig* voyage to be like a light house, meaning insightful.

London – Copyright by Steve "Mr. Pineapple" Mathieu – Picture by Hozir Sahdat

Not only does the conclusion of my research at detecting emotional patterns with more than tens of thousands of years with our timeline makes the ananas a valuable, sweet & authentic anchor but also, historically, turns out that pineapples were very useful on long boat trips because like oranges, they prevented scurvy, and it is said that pineapple juice mixed with sand is a great cleaning agent for boats. One of the 15 fundamental anchors from my conclusion is the following Mindset:

In life, no matter if it's from your own thoughts or from others, if something does not provide you with at least one of the 3, move on. You'll Thrive at becoming valuable if how you choose to think/act/speak gives Love – Time – Health and, it is often bridged with the following three: Relief a pain – Save a fear – Realistically cultivate people's ambitions & hopes. Let me please take a break of writing; I need to relief my dry throat with refreshing healthy drops of H2O … A bottle of water looks so basic but, if I purchase it at:

- the grocery store, chances are I'm going to pay $1.
- at the restaurant, I may pay $2
- at the theater, maybe $3
- at the airport, $4 for sure
- and if I'm at the Bell Center to watch the Montreal Canadians, I will need a mortgage for that same bottle of water.

This speaks of you, your products, and services because it's not that you're not valuable, but chances are that you're not in the right environment to make you valuable.

A second fundamental anchor from my conclusion is Darwin's Theory.

2025 London – Copyright by Steve "Mr. Pineapple" Mathieu – Picture by Hozir Sahdat

Darwin's theory of natural selection suggest that individuals of a species are more likely to survive in their environment and pass on their genes to the next generation when they inherit traits from their parents that are best suited for that specific environment. In this way, such traits become more widespread in the species and can lead eventually to the development of a new species. Example:

You become your surrounding because your surrounding is you.

Allow me to share a *guinea pig* experience when I exhibited with my books at 2 Bookfest in 2024. Not International Bookfairs, but Bookfest. On average, a Bookfest is a 1-day event, between 4 to 6 hours. Since 2022, I exhibit at the London Book Fair and the biggest of all, the Frankfurter Buchemesse, and I had never experimented a Bookfest.

For each, I have spent 4 to 6 hours standing tall like a pineapple at observing the small environment, and all the patterns. The surrounding was a Marketplace setting with artisan's work exhibiting what could be considered the least efforts invested. From a few basic camping tables with no tablecloth to exhibitors falling asleep on their chair, or others ignoring people passing by because their cell phone was more interesting rather than representing that they had to offer, here I was with my flashy pineapples.

When planning both projects, at first, I was pineHapply to exhibit at a cheap price compared to the luxury cost of a major Book Fair, and the environment did not fit what I was exhibiting meaning that, no matter how fruitful it looked, it did not fit the value of the people and its surrounding.

The 2 Bookfest I exhibited have confirmed, from many, the following top 3 influencers with the purpose to establish value.

First, identify your Niche.
If you think that somebody will do it, it means that nobody will do it. Applied with the purpose of marketing & selling yourself, your products, and services means that if your target is everyone, it means no one. Emotionally, I still fight this a little because The Pineapple Theory's purpose is assisting a more "pineHapply" and thriving living, together, by adding a pineapple to people's life, leadership, and business recipes. Therefore, everybody deserves a more positive living. That said, I also remember that there's more than one path to reach the top of the mountain, meaning each path to achieve a goal speaks to a niche. This application helps break through resistance from self-belief and work towards a solution.

Second, fit your environment.
Present yourself in the right environment. Darwin's Theory, again, as a Fundamental Anchor

Lastly and serving as a fruitful philosophy.
Always explore like a client, meaning experience like a *guinea pig* first because a tomato might be some fruit, but your proactive research will make you wise enough to know it must not be added into a fruit salad.

Another *guinea pig* insightful experience is from The Frankfurt Book Fair which in sum, is:

🍍 95K+ trade visitors
🍍 90K+ private visitors
🍍 4K+ exhibitors from 95 Countries

This 5-day event for which, the 3 last days are opened for the general public, inspired me at being *positively curious* with the following small experiment.

Facing my assigned booth since 2023, is a major Publisher and on the days open for the general public, many books are sold by exhibitors, and I must be very creative to poke at the visitors to distract their focus on those major publishers. For the experiment, I was selling my books 5 euro each, and because of the pineapple *mere exposure*, the representatives of the major Publisher house remember Mr. Pineapple and his ananas, and they agreed to collaborate. On their book tables, I added 5 copies of my books and marked them 10 euro each. I must share, like a pineapple placed in a mixed plate of fruits making all fruits look much more fruitful, my 5 copies truly stand out.

While I was investing passionate emotional energy at introducing my books to curious people, the 5 units at the major publisher quickly sold out without anyone needing to interact with the readers.

Harvested from the experiment is the following premium asset: Trust

With the philosophy that pineapples don't grow with magic beans, installing Trust takes time although, time can become an illusion with the knowledge that humans' emotions are built. Add sponsors to be seen or speak about you, your products, and services, and trust installs faster because you are containing several ingredients of a recipe to achieve one blooming result, and in psychology, it is referred to as *social proof,* and it suggests that people often copy the actions and opinions of others, especially when unsure of the "right" way to behave, as they assume others possess more knowledge or insight about a situation.

In perspective, a sponsor who installed Trust with their surroundings will become valuable for you as you are valuable for them.

What if I told you that Dr. Alexander Weber, a Nobel Prize winner and leading psychologist in the field of Neuroscience, has publicly recommended my must read title, The Pineapple Theory.

When people hear this, their mind does not truly question the content because it gravitates toward the credibility of Dr. Weber's Authority, the Nobel Prize in his reputation as an expert which automatically elevate the message.

It's referred to in psychology as the *authority principle,* and it suggests that people are more likely to trust and follow the guidance of those perceived as experts or authorities in a particular field, leading to compliance and acceptance of their opinions or recommendations.

The *authority principle* therefore is a power tool used to validate an idea. Once you attach an authoritative figure to a claim, the focus shifts entirely from the content to the person delivering it. Because another truth about humans' psychology is they seek the easy road, it means that most people won't dig deeper into whether the claims are true even if, like Dr. Webber, that expert doesn't exist.

Per a philosophy of The Pineapple Theory, Be Kind & Truthful and life will be Fruitful, meaning always do the right things for the right things to happen to you because reality is always waiting to hit back.

Like clusters of flowers grouping to form the pineapple fruit when growing in the right environment, the content of this book is currently grouping like this chapter also will assemble all together. But first, allow me the share a serving of history about the pineapple.

History suggests that it was Christopher Columbus who brought the pineapple to Europe. Records reveal that in 1493, the friendly inhabitants of the Antilles Island of Guadeloupe welcomed the foreign traveler with this exotic fruit. Columbus was so enamored with its taste that he took it home with him.

In addition to serving as food, with its natural sweetness, the pineapple has served in history as a symbol and an artistic motif. The rarity, reputation, expense, and visual attractiveness of the pineapple made it an item of celebrity and the "ultimate exotic fruit." The pineapple was so coveted and uncommon that in 1677, King Charles II of England posed receiving a pineapple as a gift in an official portrait, a symbolic act viewed of royal privilege.

2024 Scotland – Copyright by Steve "Mr. Pineapple" Mathieu – Picture by Olga Tyukova

The pineapple became a symbol of hospitality and served as the pinnacle of an entertaining household's feast, even being rented to households during the day for display on the table and then sold to more affluent clients who ate it.

Explaining why I today travel the world to write my book and walk cities while carrying casually a pineapple fruit is because 17th century Londoners were renting the jewel of the jungle for 5,000 British Pounds, casually carrying it only to show off and being proud to say that they can offer such an exotic fruit.

As a symbol of hospitality and friendship, the pineapple became a favorite motif of architects, artisans, and craftsman in the American colonies, and would be seen on the main gate posts of mansions, in the weathervanes of public buildings, and on walls, canvas mats, tablecloths, napkins, the backs of chairs, and so forth.

Even St-Paul's did not escape it, and if you visit London, take quality time to observe the pineapple shining high.

2025 London – Copyright by Steve "Mr. Pineapple" Mathieu – Picture by Hozir Sahdat

Niche – Environment – Sponsor - Figure of Authority - Mere exposure - Trust - Giving Love-Time-Health / Relief pain – Save a fear – Support ambitions & hopes - Limited or Rarity.

They are all ingredients in the recipe that made a pineapple valuable. Because it requires more than one anchor to navigate your boat of life, becoming valuable can easily become a complex recipe because once again, humans' emotions are built, not just felt, and humans are hard wired to their primitive behaviors define as Size, Object, Location, Distance, Motion, Orientation, Sound, Physiology, Emotions, Color, and People.

Learn everything easily about these primitive behavior with title, *The Tangled Mind,* by Nick Kolenda. He did awesome at explaining each.

Inspiring enlightening insights with the purpose to encoding humans at better defining their worth gives value to one's *positive curiosity* with a consultant, and books. Though, no matter how many books you may read, if you don't know how to use them nor consistent at practicing, it worth nothing.

What if people could Thrive more pineHapply by adding a pineapple to their life, leadership, and business recipes?

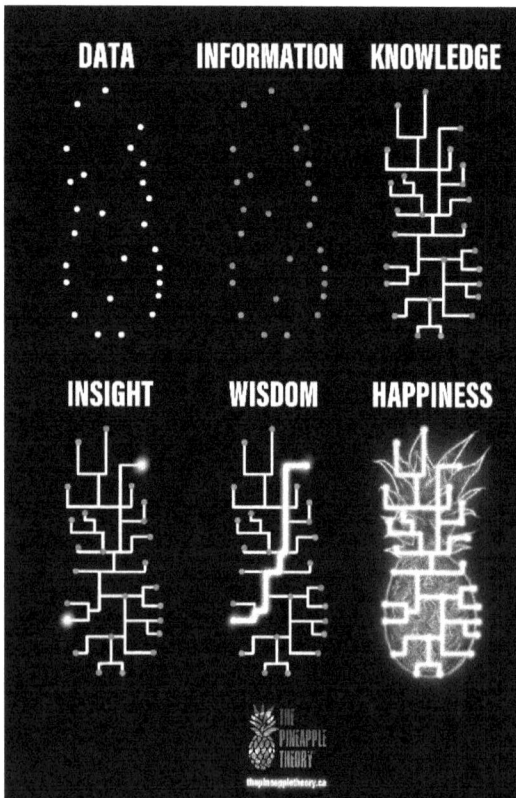

Surveyed by The Pineapple Theory

How often do you impulsively purchase on Amazon and realize you did not need it once received?

43%: Never
31%: I stopped counting!
17%: At least once a month
9%: People around me, yes.

IS IT
PINEAPPLE
WORLDWIDE?

Overview

Like me, maybe you operate by yourself. Maybe you achieved a decent amount of revenue and now need to build a team, meaning adding more farmers to grow your products and services. No matter if it is by yourself or with a team, is it pineapple worldwide?

Several expanding corporate companies hope for consistency, referred to as standardization across the board. Starting on good growing soil requires training programs, Standard Operational Procedures (SOP), and Policies. Each must bridge with the culture and be nicely written and coached. If you contract an author with a global vision and with an understanding of processes because they have, for example, a Lean Six Sigma belt, the seed will be nicely planted.

Don't do like many entrepreneurs starting to grow and managing damage control because they lacked vision with this one. It will not be perfect, but you will have a foundation, and it will always keep improving. With a foundation, change is more efficient and less painful to influence. Still searching my text journal, the following inspiration was found and nicely fits with this chapter.

A brand is everything for a company; logo, purpose, and how it pinches people's heart & mind must inspire trust for customers, it must be a sign of consistency and a worldwide standard.

Story

In 2022, one week prior to my flight to Frankfurt (DE), I shipped myself a parcel to the hotel where I've booked, and I have top tier status with that chain loyalty program. The parcel was confirmed received by the General Manager five days prior to my check-in date.

I arrived at the hotel, and when completing the checking process, I was told my parcel was shipped to the wrong hotel of that same chain located approximately at a 20-minutes walking distance, and I will need to pick it up myself.

I applied my *positive curiosity* although my *emotional batteries* felt low following an over night flight and time zone change. Also, cleverly shared with my theory, are the following 3 big troublemakers for one's emotional focus shutting down the bridge to our thinking, just like a child:

🍍 Sleepy
🍍 Hungry
🍍 Urgent need to do peepee!

Yes, all 3 were striking me at the time, meaning that I needed to be the master of my emotions, and I asked:

"I'm positively curious to learn if there were any roadblock for someone to bring the parcel here, knowing there was a mistake with the delivery?"

Their response was:

"In several other countries, they would done it before your arrival. Here in Germany, don't expect this type of experience."

Along with supporting corporate companies with their brand for 25+ years, I have my own with The Pineapple Theory, and their response felt like a slap to my face. Self-control is preventing being slave to our emotions. Your reaction to what is negative will exhibit your truest character and remember that people will always remember how you made them feel followed by the 1:250 rule. All I could respond with a positive tone was:

"It should not be about the Country. It should shadow about what is the brand shown behind you, on the wall, when guests enter the Hotel."

What do you think? What can we harvest from this experience?

Let's harvest and reflect.

Because I understand there is no perfection in life, my experience was an exception when compared to my guest experience with this hotel chain. I simply moved on, shared constructive feedback with the

General Manager, and booked another Hotel of that same chain for future Frankfurt projects.

But what about a first-time guest?
A first-time guest would fall under the 1%-3% of emotional buyers which become Schrödinger's Cat.

Remaining positive and consistent with ourselves is already challenging in life, imagine when you must influence that same positive and inner growth with a team. Leadership is not only a job, but also a commitment and responsibility like being a parent. Leading by example will always start with you, and it must embody you.

Surveyed by The Pineapple Theory

Which is often a top 3 first asked question by an interviewer?

30%: Why you?
26%: Why us?
26%: What is your biggest accomplishment?
17%: Salary expectation

When asked about your experience with projects at a job interview, should your personal life projects count and/or be considered?

60%: Yes, it's a project.
20%: No.
20%: Interesting perspective.

VITAMINS
OF THE
PINEAPPLE!

We are approaching the end of this book, and you may have a few sticky notes between pages along with highlighted sentences. If you close the book and carefully observe the effect of each sticky note, they are like a ladder. That is an analogy exhibiting what reading books does. Your growth is like climbing each step of a ladder, 1-by-1, leading beyond the limits of the universe with your inspirations. The more you stack books, the higher the ladder.

I shared with you several perspectives about the type of farmer you can become. When you plant a seed and cultivate it, you do not only harvest revenue, but you also become happier with yourself, more prosperous as a salesperson, and a more engaging leader because you are earning people's heart. Remember that achieving your goals is not as important as what you become by achieving them.

With the knowledge that everything in life must come to an end, one day, you will exit your business. You may not have the ability to predict a future that does not exist, but nothing stops you from working towards your goals. On your path, the road to get there may change. My question to you is, how would you like to exit?

Even when I self-reflect about this, it struck my mind that in 25+ years of corporate experience for example, I never resigned. I moved to a different company because of lay-offs giving volume to one treasure hardly found with current generations: Loyalty.

Nevertheless, like in show business, always leave on a high note. That is how many are positively remembered and wanted for more. Following small edits fitting this book, here's a motivational text full of vitamins of the pineapple extracted from my title, *The Pineapple Theory,* with the purpose of loving a pineapple with an inner roar.

If you want to live a life most people don't, my question to you is, are you ready to do what most people don't?

Albert Einstein
There are only two ways to live your life. One is as though nothing is a miracle. The other is as though everything is a miracle.

One's accomplishment can inspire one. It is a pattern, a cycle. A purpose takes birth. It triggers ambitions and goals. There are Ups & Downs. And it ends with an accomplishment. And accomplishment is not about luck.

Don't wait for life to change you because life is the one waiting for you to change. Therefore, don't wait to be harvested, build your own path. The path is within. Do not be afraid of new beginnings. Let the seed of a new purpose trigger your ambitions and goals. Cultivate a growth continuum. Cultivate your seed for greatness.

Keep a strong mind

Don't expect fast results.
Don't stop believing in yourself.
Don't get stuck in the past.
Don't dwell on mistakes.
Don't fear the future.
Don't resist change.
Don't give up on your superpowers.
Don't let your weaknesses take control of your mind.
Don't feel like the world owes you something.
Don't fear failure, more than you desire success.
Understand the value of a proper work/life balance.
Don't assume that your problems are unique.
Don't see failure as a signal to turn back.
Don't feel sorry for yourself.
Never give up on yourself.

Believe to Achieve

The limits of your ambitions and goals, do not let them be the making of your own mind. Giving up is only when accepting to be defeated in your mind. Never limit your ambitions. Sky's limit is not enough. Go beyond the limits of the universe.

Never give up

In life, you will never speak to anyone than you speak to yourself in your mind – therefore - it is important to be kind to yourself. If you're not waiting and doing something, it does not matter how things might be at first because you're still way ahead of everyone who isn't even trying.

No *plateau,* no *status quo*

Unless you take at least one definite step forward, you'll never get something done. One step forward leads to thousands of steps forward. Daily, you take at least one step forward, for many things. Do the same with your ambitions and goals. When we have ambitions and goals, it means that we are passionate about them, and working for passion is an amazing feeling. Take that one first step forward. In life, remember that some will give up due to slow progress.

Because pineapples don't grow with magic beans, never grasp the fact that slow progress is progress. It does not matter how fast you move if you never stop, like an ananas growing tiny millimeters at the time. Look back from time to time from where you started and acknowledge the milestones you've reached and recognize them. You've earned them and they were harvested from your hard work and if there's a sit back, never give up. After all, if you have a flat tire on your vehicle, would you slash all 3 remaining tires?

Surround yourself with people who encourage and push you to succeed. People who will recognize your milestones as if they were theirs.

To aim for something, you must have a target. Give yourself small objectives to give yourself small recognition because that's how you eat a full pineapple, one bite at a time. You'll be committed. The remaining steps will be completed with great passion. There's nothing more beautiful than when you prove to yourself just how strong you are.

You will grow by facing challenges. Don't limit your challenges – rather – challenge your limits! Difficult doesn't mean impossible like pineapples that once grew in the unfit climate of the UK in the 16th century. Everything you find easy today was from a place of incomfort.

Stay focus

There will be pain from time to time. Optimism is a happiness magnet. Do the right things and the right things will happen to you. Keep speaking positively to yourself. It will become your gain.

No Pain No Gain

Enjoy the accomplishment that will inspire someone else. Because one's accomplishment can inspire one. It is a pattern, a cycle. A purpose takes birth. It triggers ambitions and goals. There are Ups & Downs. And it ends with an accomplishment. And accomplishment is not about luck.

Don't wait for life to change you because life is the one waiting for you to change.

Surveyed by The Pineapple Theory

Do you have the courage to leave your job to become an entrepreneur?

44%: No
21%: Yes, I'm getting ready for it.
18%: I did and it's tough.
18%: I did and no regrets, love it!

TPT
BOOK
COLLECTION

PineHapply Thrive like a Pineapple!
thepineappletheory.ca

WHY the pineapple?

WORLDWIDE FRUITFUL TRAVELS WITH A PINEAPPLE

Mr. Pineapple

Legend of the Thousa... PiÑa the AnaNas

MR. PINEAPPLE

Available on
amazon

WHAT is The Pineapple Theory?

THE PINEAPPLE THEORY™

Mr. Pineapple

Uncover forgotten golden parts
of you to become the
thriving leader you deserve.

THE
PINEAPPLE
THEORY™

Mr. Pineapple

THE PINEAPPLE THEORY™

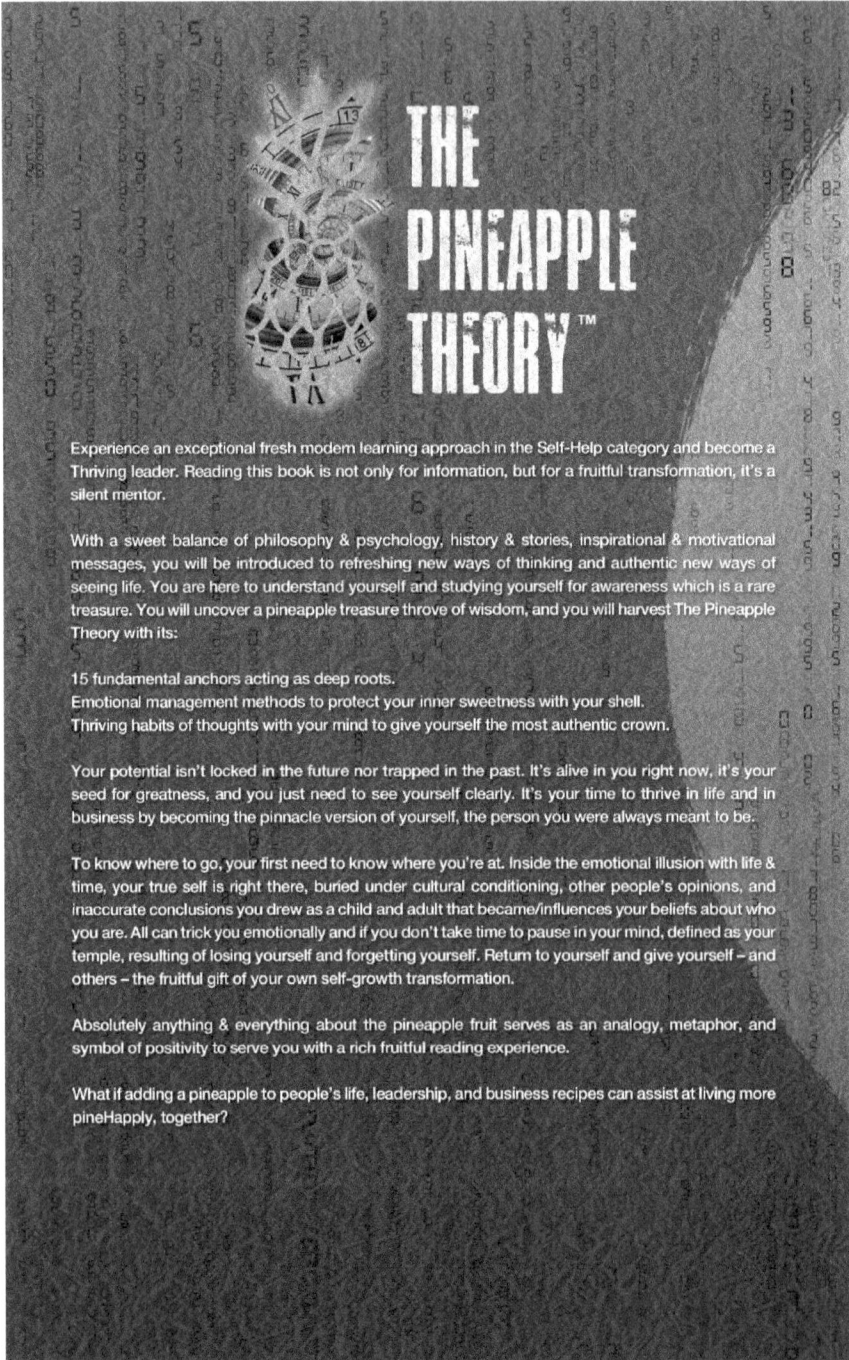

Experience an exceptional fresh modern learning approach in the Self-Help category and become a Thriving leader. Reading this book is not only for information, but for a fruitful transformation, it's a silent mentor.

With a sweet balance of philosophy & psychology, history & stories, inspirational & motivational messages, you will be introduced to refreshing new ways of thinking and authentic new ways of seeing life. You are here to understand yourself and studying yourself for awareness which is a rare treasure. You will uncover a pineapple treasure throve of wisdom, and you will harvest The Pineapple Theory with its:

15 fundamental anchors acting as deep roots.
Emotional management methods to protect your inner sweetness with your shell.
Thriving habits of thoughts with your mind to give yourself the most authentic crown.

Your potential isn't locked in the future nor trapped in the past. It's alive in you right now, it's your seed for greatness, and you just need to see yourself clearly. It's your time to thrive in life and in business by becoming the pinnacle version of yourself, the person you were always meant to be.

To know where to go, your first need to know where you're at. Inside the emotional illusion with life & time, your true self is right there, buried under cultural conditioning, other people's opinions, and inaccurate conclusions you drew as a child and adult that became/influences your beliefs about who you are. All can trick you emotionally and if you don't take time to pause in your mind, defined as your temple, resulting of losing yourself and forgetting yourself. Return to yourself and give yourself – and others – the fruitful gift of your own self-growth transformation.

Absolutely anything & everything about the pineapple fruit serves as an analogy, metaphor, and symbol of positivity to serve you with a rich fruitful reading experience.

What if adding a pineapple to people's life, leadership, and business recipes can assist at living more pineHapply, together?

Cooking - History - Health Benefits
Travel Activities - and the ultimate proof that
life & humans are amazingly pineapple

WORLDWIDE FRUITFUL TRAVELS WITH A PINEAPPLE

Mr. Pineapple

"Mr. Pineapple, why the pineapple?"

With the purpose to inspire everyone to live more "pineHapply", I travel the world to write my books, I carefully observed more than tens of thousands of years with our history to detect emotional patterns, and hands-down, "why the pineapple" is the most asked question.

Absolutely everything about the pineapple fruit serves as an analogy, metaphor, and symbol of positivity making one's reading of *The Pineapple Theory™* book series about philosophy much more fruitful. For many, this answer is for from enough because in life, nothing will ever be enough. So, I embarked into a 5-year journey & research for which, I pulled the string of our timeline about the pineapple as much as possible until the roots could not be seen anymore.

Following 15+ Countries along with 9 photographers and 5 Chefs, I present to you this one of kind hybrid book like a pineapple standing tall in a mixed plate of fruits:

- You will discover the amazing history of the pineapple fruit.
- You will discover peculiar pineapple landmarks and unique pineapple travel attractions.
- Pictures from worldwide freelance photographers I support when I travel.
- Exclusive to this book, easy to make food & drink recipes by Chefs.
- You will discover several pineapple health benefits.
- You'll enjoy the infamous kinkiness of the pineapple.
- Lastly, serving as a fundamental for upcoming lectures and motivational speeches on stage, I will share my moving and powerful story about my Author-Preneurship venture about this 5-year journey bridged with my collection of The Pineapple Theory books, and the conclusions of my research about life and humans.

Following your reading, not only will you realize how amazingly pineapple Earth, Life, and Humans are, but you will better understand the philosophical purpose of *The Pineapple Theory™*:

Theoretically, what if adding a pineapple to people's life, leadership, and business recipes can assist living more "pineHapply", together?

Sorry, not sorry, you will never see a pineapple the same way again, or yourself, or both!

Enjoy *The Pineapple Theory™*'s savory gold standard for more "pineHappliness!"

Inspired by the Filippino Urban Legend in the book, *Worldwide fruitful travels with a pineapple,* harvest a refreshing and sweet modern approach of The Pina with a Thousand Eyes, speaking how less addicted time on our electronic devices cultivates more acts of kindness towards others, and ourselves.

Also available in Deutch thanks to and available for your projects.

ARTIST
OF
VALUE

When I travel to investigate our emotional timeline with more than tens of thousands of years of trackable history, I always establish partnership with a local freelance photographer, and their art inspires me daily with thousands of words. My books are my evidence, from each travel and several pictures, most of my manuscripts are inspired by, and speak of the pictures inserted in the books giving life to the following English proverb; an image speak a thousand words. That's thanks to each photographer.

I truly admire what they do, they labor hard at continuously improving the growth quality of their art, and at improving themselves as humans. They understand the art of cultivating the greatness of a positive experience. Let them show·you with their art, the greatness living within.

thepineappletheory.ca

London, United Kingdom

Hozir Sadhat, Hozz Photo, is a photographer and videographer based in London, and his multimedia creations helps brands and individuals stand out through visual arts.

Hozir has experience in many different sectors of photography including fashion, lifestyle, and product photography, with the main goal to provide brands/individuals that wish to stand out from the crowd.

https://hozzphoto.com/

Edinburgh, Scotland

Olga Tjukova is an Edinburgh-based commercial photographer, working for local businesses, charities, universities, museums, and private clients. She provides a range of services including interior design, products, and event photography, as well as portraiture.

www.papajka.com

Athens, Greece

Georgios Makkas is an Athens based photographer and videographer incorporating into his work, various styles of photography.

Specializing in editorial and portrait photography, Georgios delivers high end imagery and always focuses on the human aspect when sharing a story with his work.

https://www.gmakkas.com/index

Germany

Marc Maria started using a camera when he was fifteen years old. For him, the camera is a fountain pen, it writes a story and sentences in contrast and soft tones. This moment, this photographic moment is about intention, it's about you and how amazing you are, because a person who shines is a good person.

Marc wishes to photograph as many people as possible, show them how interesting they are, how unique they are, and give them something they can share.

https://www.marcmaria.de/

Tokyo, Japan

Yusuke Harada is a Japanese photographer based in Tokyo. He has photographed the world's major conflicts and its hidden crisis. After studying Digital imaging technique in professional school in Japan, he traveled around the world, such as Palestine, Iraq, Sudan, Angola, and some Asian countries.

He started his career as a professional photographer when he had traveled and photographed in Pakistan for three months in 2009. Since then, he has independently photographed and documented throughout Africa, Middle East, and Asia.

He changed his base from Tokyo to Cairo in Egypt since 2012 to start his long-term project: the aftermath of the Arab Spring, covering the ongoing conflicts in various Middle East countries, especially Syria and Egypt. He was back to Japan in 2015.

His works have received several awards, grants, and have been published in several magazines and newspapers in Japan and other countries.

https://yusukeharada.com/work

Montreal (Quebec/Canada)

Annie Langlois is a photographer with a true passion for people. For her, the art of photography is an exceptional and privileged way to connect with people and their stories because life is made of people, moments, and emotions to cherish. Annie is a social butterfly by nature and everyone she meets makes her art continuously grow.

https://www.annielangloisphotographe.com/

Cairo, Egypt

Mostafa Yousef's passion for photography and purpose of making everyone feel prettier with themselves, build self-confidence, and make great memories started when he was 17 years old.

He captured a picture of a friend, and they shared to Yousef that they felt prettier with the camera's eyes. The feedback became an inspiration to self-taught, practice, and truly be the best at using his camera. Yousef specializes in Portrait, Fashion, and Wedding photography.

https://www.behance.net/t2yousef1/

Hong Kong

Óscar Cordeiro is a passionate Portuguese photographer based in Hong Kong, and he loves capturing the essence of what surrounds him.

The name RACSO comes from a symbolic expression suggesting the other side of the lens; him behind the camera viewfinder. At first, he viewed it as a joke and as time passed, and he kept the name to exhibit himself photographically.

Always nurturing his passion for photography, Oscar excels with several genres such as landscape, documentary, and street photography. No matter what you have in mind, and it's more magical for the things you have not thought about, Oscar will capture his passion for you.

https://www.racsophoto.com/